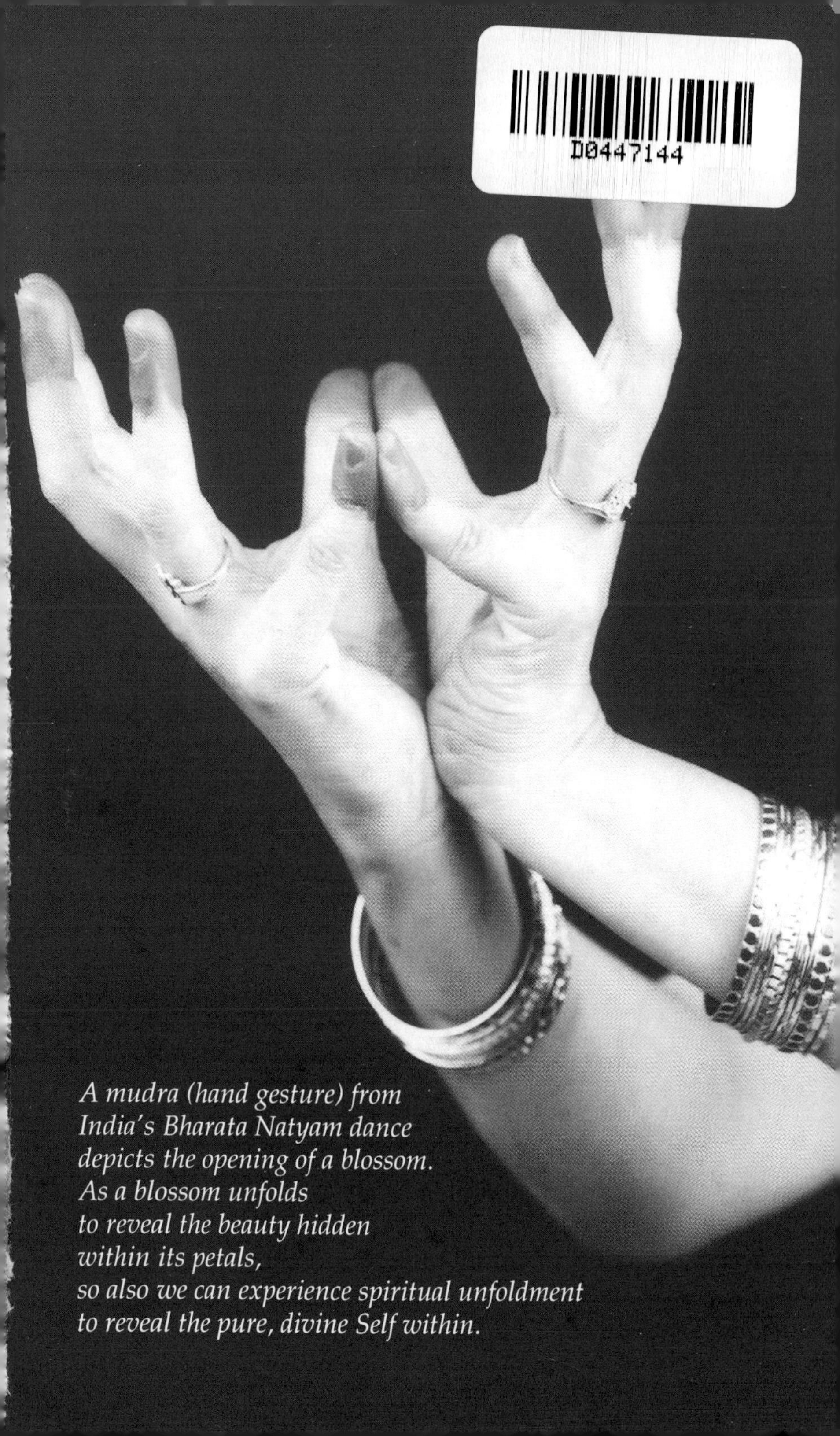

A mudra (hand gesture) from India's Bharata Natyam dance depicts the opening of a blossom. As a blossom unfolds to reveal the beauty hidden within its petals, so also we can experience spiritual unfoldment to reveal the pure, divine Self within.

THE *Self-Discovery* SERIES

Meditation and Life

Self-Unfoldment

Self- Unfoldment

Sailesh & Smitha
March 2nd, 2008
Lincoln High School,
San Jose

THE *Self-Discovery* SERIES

Self-Unfoldment

New Edition

By
SWAMI CHINMAYANANDA

CHINMAYA PUBLICATIONS

Chinmaya Publications
Main Office
P.O. Box 129
Piercy, CA 95587, USA

Chinmaya Publications
Distribution Office
560 Bridgetown Pike
Langhorne, PA 19053

Central Chinmaya Mission Trust
Sandeepany Sadhanalaya
Saki Vihar Road
Bombay, India 400 072

Printed in the United States of America

Second Printing 1994

Earlier editions of the present work have been published as *Manual of Self-Unfoldment:* First published in Napa, California, by Chinmaya Publications West in 1975. Subsequently published and reprinted in India by Central Chinmaya Mission Trust in 1976, 1977, 1981, 1983, 1985, and 1987.

Credits:

Cover design by Peter Tucker
Photo of Swami Chinmayananda on the back cover
by Joy Von Tiedemann
Photo of blossoms on the cover by Bill Browning
Photo of Swami Chinmayananda on page iv by Anjli Singh
Photo of dancer's hands on page i courtesy of Nandini Rangan

Library of Congress Catalog Card Number 92-74652

Contents

Foreword

Have you ever asked yourself these questions:

- Who am I — really?
- Where did I come from? Where was I before I was born? Where will I be after I die?
- Why am I sometimes happy, sometimes sad?
- Am I OK as I am, or should I be something else?
- Why does the world sometimes scream at me, sometimes smile at me?
- Does it really make a difference whether I tell a lie or not?
- Why do I always seem to want just a little more than I have?

Self-Unfoldment helps us answer those questions — and many more. But before you start reading, imagine this:

Imagine what it would be like to be always happy — perfectly satisfied with the way things are. You gaze around your room, and every object in it seems to be vibrant with life. From the books on the shelf to the plant by the window, everything is in its place and as it should be. Everything belongs to a beautiful, harmonious whole of which you are also a part. You feel connected, happy, complete. The car you hear through the window, revving up its engines unnecessarily, does not disturb you in the least. The dog barking in the neighbor's yard sounds happy, a part of your cheerful world. Nothing has the power to upset you. Nothing can be added to your world to make it better. It is perfect as it is.

It's possible to feel this happy and whole all the time. Those who have become enlightened beings know this uninterrupted happiness and completeness as part of their every breathing minute. In fact, everyone of us — including you who are reading this page — are already happy and whole, except that we do not know it. We need to undo some of the wrong thought patterns we've developed — and once those are undone, we can experience greater happiness than we ever even dreamed of.

The pages that follow are a compilation of the writings and transcribed talks of Swami Chinmayananda, one of the foremost teachers of Vedanta of our times. As he unfolds the teaching, he reveals to us the path to our own inner unfoldment.

Rudite Emir

Preface

If a newborn baby, entering into this world of endless space all around it, suffers from the crushing atmospheric pressure and therefore feels lost — even more poignant are the confusions and discomforts that a seeker feels when he first enters into the spiritual world. He has left the comforts of his egocentered, desire-prompted, lust-seeking world, issuing from his own sense of ownership and vanity. However, he has not yet arrived in the world of understanding, let alone experienced the rhythm of the divine Self.

As the child grows and picks up more understanding of the world around him, he becomes increasingly at ease with the seemingly endless world of things and beings. Similarly, the seeker can discover his inner peace and joyous enthusiasm only when he continues his diligent inquiry and learns to perceive the logical rhythm of the apparently crazy confusion of happenings around him.

"Life is a tragedy to those who feel; life is a comedy to those who think," sings the poet, and it is true. In order to understand Nature and her behavior, material scientists for centuries have been observing and studying the objective phenomena of the world. The ancient rishis (sages or seers) pursued a different system of study: They turned their attention to the subjective Self and studied the world around them from that subjective standpoint. This subjective study constitutes the Science of Reality (*brahmavidyā*), the theme and content of Vedanta.

Great sages and saints from the Vedic days onward have been doing research on this silent and mysterious inner world. We have to bring their discoveries and conclusions within the ambit of our own direct experience; otherwise, the science would not be a subjective one, remaining only as a set of objective and rational pieces of information and conclusions.

In the long, tiresome stretch of time, masters in various generations "woke up" to realize the pure Self as the ultimate truth in themselves. To move us from our present state of consciousness into this immaculate, nondual substratum for the Einsteinian world of change, we have to bring about some essential changes in the inner composition of our personality. These techniques and methods constitute yoga.

We, the product of the modern age of science and technology, cannot accept this subjective science as our forefathers could, in their faith and deep devotion to the tradition of Vedanta. To provide the necessary intellectual props to build up at least a thin veneer of faith in the possibility of the mind-transcending state of perfection declared by Vedanta, in this book I have tried to offer the logic of Self-unfoldment.

This book was published earlier in India as the *Manual of Self-Unfoldment*. Rudite Emir has edited it and has added very useful pages in this American edition, including analogies heard at many of my lectures over the years. I thank her for amending each chapter with a section for the reader's study and reflection and for adding a special charm and attraction to the entire text. I feel extremely grateful to her for the rich gift she has provided for our modern society.

I recommend this book as a very essential text for the spiritual seeker who, once he masters the content, will feel no further obstacles in his sincere pursuit of the spiritual life.

Chinmayananda
Allendale, Michigan
July 1992

Freedom 1

The world is a glorious place to live in. Nature provides us with food, sunshine, rain, and a wealth of plants, animals, and minerals. The phenomenal powers, which have been threatening and persecuting humankind for millennia, have been largely tamed and harnessed to serve humanity. People have grown from a primitive and barbarous state to become a civilized and intelligent society. In this day and age, we enjoy many comforts of life, even luxuries. The comforts we enjoy are almost heavenly, and we have become used to indulging in them without the least restraint.

But are we happy?

Most of us are not happy — at least not fully so or all of the time. We sit amid our wealth and comforts and live lives of worry, anxiety, and dissatisfaction. Somehow, we never feel quite satisfied. This paradox makes up our lives.

Great thinkers over the years have analyzed this paradox in order to find a way to lasting happiness. They discovered that the mind becomes unhappy when we try to satisfy *every* desire that comes into it. In fact, satisfying every desire can, in time, lead to much unhappiness.

> This fact can be illustrated through simple examples from life. For instance, the first helping of our favorite ice cream is a great joy; the second helping still brings much enjoyment. But if we continue eating ice-cream cone after ice-cream cone, we'll find that that which at first brought us great pleasure is now making us literally sick.

As a result of such observations, the great thinkers of the world defined certain basic guidelines for living, in order to help people gain a deeper and more lasting happiness.

Our essential nature is freedom. We therefore resist any shackles on our personality. We don't like being told what to do or not to do. So we revolt against any rules or guidelines that restrain us in any way. We do not realize that true freedom is built on intelligent self-restraint.

> For instance, when we drive a car, our freedom of movement on the highway is subject to the discipline of following traffic rules. If these rules are not followed, the movement of vehicles on the road will be totally out of control, leading to chaos.

The Art of Right Contact

The laws of a country protect the freedom of its people but prevent them from being reckless and irresponsible in their activities. In a similar way, religious books prescribe a code of conduct for life that gives us a means for developing and maintaining the right contact with the world. If we learn to follow such a code intelligently, we can lead a healthy and dynamic life.

> We as consumers of electricity have the freedom to use it in our homes in any way we wish: from toasting our bread to powering our stereo. But in order to benefit from the power of electricity, we have to maintain a proper relationship to it — the right contact. For instance, we better not plug in an appliance with wet fingers, nor poke nails into electrical outlets. If we choose not to follow these guidelines, the outcome will be simple: we'll die. The same power that blesses can also destroy us — if we don't maintain the right contact to it.

A general complaint among people is that the world is full of evil and problems. And they ask:

"How can I find peace and happiness?"

The religious masters of the world have, time and again, answered this question by explaining that peace and happiness do not exist in the external world, but are generated within ourselves when we maintain proper contact with the world.

In fact, our problems in life are a blessing in disguise, since they help perfect our personality — *if* we apply the art of right contact.

> As a rule, we use a rough surface to sharpen a blunt instrument. For example, we use the roughness of a grindstone to sharpen a knife — provided that we apply the knife correctly to the grindstone, at the right angle, for the right amount of time. Similarly, our personality gets "sharpened," or chastened, amid the problems of life — if we have learned to maintain the proper contact with the world.

The scriptures provide guidelines for us to maintain the proper relationship to the world. If we don't follow those guidelines, we maintain the wrong contact and complain of a bad world. No doubt, the world is a mixture of good and bad, but we can learn the knack of using the rough edges of experience to perfect our personality. If we don't develop that knack, the roughness of the world will blunt our personality instead. We will become bitter and ever more deeply unhappy.

We cannot blame the world for our unhappy state of mind. Not the world, but *our view of it,* is what determines our state of mind.

> Take the case of a glass half-filled with milk. One person looks at the empty upper half and complains that the glass is half-*empty,* while another sees the milk in the bottom half and is happy that the glass if half-*full.*
>
> The pessimist always sees the bad side of life (the empty

> portion of the glass) and worries over it, while the optimist sees the brighter side of each situation (the full portion of the glass) and enjoys it.

We first must learn to be grateful for what we have. Such an attitude brings about mental tranquillity. When our minds are tranquil, our faculties are alert and our actions effective. In contrast, when our minds are agitated with desires to get something we do not have, we lose not only our peace of mind, but also our concentration and our efficiency in action.

> A lame man in a wheelchair despairs at the sight of a healthy pair of legs moving past him. But the owner of those fast-moving legs sighs as he watches another man swiftly passing him on a motorcycle. The man on the motorcycle is, in turn, jealous of the smartly dressed woman driving by in the latest model of his favorite-make car. The car owner, though, is not happy either. She's worried about her huge tax bill for the year.

All this misery can be stopped by taking the first step: developing a sense of gratitude for what we have, which many less fortunate than us are denied. This idea can be summarized by the old saying:

> *I had no shoes and complained — until I met a man who had no feet.*

Our Heritage

Independence is the very essence of being a human. The person who has become free from his slave-like dependence upon the world is truly free. Such a person does not depend on the world to provide joy. The person who has not learned to live in such independence is tossed back and forth by the problems of life — much like an abandoned boat in a stormy sea.

Vedanta, the science of Self-unfoldment, teaches us how to regain our divine heritage, to become beings who are free of all dependence on the world, having rediscovered the unchanging, blissful nature of their true Self.

> In the literature of Vedanta,[1] the world is frequently compared to the ocean. The surface of the ocean is made up of an infinite variety of waves forever rising and falling. Although the surface is restless, deep within, the same ocean remains serene and unaffected by the surface disturbances.
>
> Similarly, when we look at the world superficially, it has a variety of objects and beings that are continually changing, being born and dying. However, behind these changing forms is a changeless substratum — the all-pervading Reality supporting them all.

Today, we tend to live mainly on the surface of our existence. We are busy with the changing objects and events. We identify with these changes, becoming joyous one moment and unhappy the next. We are slaves to those changes. If, however, we learned to identify ourselves with the unchanging Reality behind those changes, we would rise above those ups and downs of daily living and would learn to enjoy lasting happiness.

An enlightened being is one who has gained mastery over his own mind, who is always at peace no matter what changes may be taking place in the world around him. At times, others mistake such a person for being indifferent and disinterested in the world. The truth is, however, that the enlightened person experiences emotions, but he does not let them overpower him. Such a person *has* an emotion, but does not *become* the emotion; he does not become emotional.

---

[1] Vedanta is the science of life developed over thousands of years by the ancient masters of India. The word hails from *veda + anta*, "the end of the Vedas," Vedanta being the essence of the Upanishads, a collection of sacred texts found at the end of each of the four Vedas. Vedanta comprises the philosophic principles underlying all of the major religions of the world. See Chapter 15, "Vedanta," for a detailed discussion of Vedanta.

The human being consists of a body, a mind, and an intellect — and the Life Principle, which gives life to these three kinds of equipment. The body-mind-intellect equipment functions in the following areas of experience:

The body	in the realm of perceptions and actions
The mind	in the realm of emotions
The intellect	in the realm of thoughts and ideas

There's nothing wrong in our using the body and the senses to perceive and act, but we should not let ourselves get *caught up* in our perceptions and actions. Again, there's no problem with feeling emotions, but we should not be overwhelmed by them. At the intellectual level, we can entertain thoughts and ideas, but we should not let ourselves be driven by them. If we thus learn to stand apart from the influence of perceptions-emotions-thoughts, we become truly independent in life.

Such freedom is our heritage as human beings.

For Your Study and Reflection

1. Freedom

STUDY QUESTIONS, Level 1

1. Describe some experiences in your own life that illustrate how too much of a good thing became unpleasant for you. What does this teach you about striving to satisfy every desire you entertain in your mind?

2. Recall an experience in your life in which your attitude toward an event changed the way you felt about that event. Did your attitude make you feel stronger or weaker? More happy or more sad? Why?

3. Take a moment to feel grateful about something in your life. Watch your mind as you entertain thoughts of gratitude. What happens to your mind?

STUDY QUESTIONS, Level 2

1. Describe the difference between inner independence and the freedom that a nation's laws may grant us.

2. How does a sense of gratitude help calm our minds? What attitude is the opposite of gratitude, and what effect does it have on our minds?

3. Describe the difference in attitude of an enlightened being and an unenlightened one in reference to life's changing circumstances.

FOR YOUR REFLECTION

- Many wrong habits of thinking and acting enter into us unconsciously. They thrive in their secret lush growth to form dangerous jungles of weeds in which lurk poisonous serpents of disastrous tendencies. These unseen foes raise their hoods, hiss, and strike us from behind when we are at the heat of our activities, engaged fully in meeting our problems in life. Let us never allow such thorny undergrowths to thrive in our bosom. It is suicidal. (Swami Chinmayananda, *We Must*, page 50)

- By our own thoughts . . . we are the architects of our own manifestations. If we cultivate our thoughts to be dynamic and positive, we have cultivated ourselves. In every moment we are somehow trying to gratify our wants, fulfill our desires, satisfy our needs, express our ideas, and accomplish our ideals. Yet we know that all wants, desires, needs, ideas, and ideals are nothing but thoughts. Taming the thoughts is taming the personality . . . (Swami Chinmayananda, *We Must*, page 32)

FURTHER READING

- Swami Chinmayananda, *We Must*. Napa, California: Chinmaya Publications West, 1976. Chapters 13-15.

Happiness 2

All human activities are motivated by two impulses:

- Revulsion to sorrow (*duḥkha nivṛtti*)[1]
- Yearning for joy (*sukha prāpti*)

All of the so-called milestones in the history of human progress are nothing but victories over a particular source of unhappiness or an overcoming of a limitation imposed on us by Nature. A closer look at all human discoveries, starting from the making of the first fire by prehistoric man to the splitting of the atom, a space flight, or a heart transplant in the modern world, are nothing but milestones in our flight from sorrow and our rush toward joy.

The Joy of Living

This exodus from discomfort and anxious rush toward comfort form the basis for what we generally call our attempts to establish a higher standard of living.[2] Pursuit of these two

[1] Wherever appropriate, the concept under discussion is translated into the original Sanskrit used in the ancient texts of Vedanta. For further details on the Sanskrit language and on Vedanta terminology, see "Guide to Sanskrit Transliteration and Pronunciation" and the Glossary.

[2] See Chapter 4, "Balance," for further discussion of this topic.

objectives (avoiding discomfort, seeking comfort) at the collective level is the task of all governments and nations. The politicians, economists, and scientists are all trying their best to rearrange the pattern of the outer world in an attempt to eliminate sorrow and provide for happiness. But the sad fact remains that no established pattern in the outer world of things and beings can remain steadily unchanged in a prearranged condition for any length of time. Also impossible is to find a suitable arrangement of the outer world to meet the various demands of an innumerable variety of human beings on the face of this earth. Therefore, in spite of all the best efforts at planning by secular governments and material scientists, our lives remain riddled with discomforts and sorrows, poverty and strife. Thus, wars and revolutions still continue.

At the individual level, we are constantly busy avoiding all things disagreeable to us and pursuing all things agreeable. However, since the objects around us and the environment are constantly changing, we are kept endlessly busy trying to keep an acceptable balance of favorable factors in our lives. We may succeed for a while, but then again fall into a state of dissatisfaction.

> You pine for long months for the perfect job, and it finally arrives: a successful firm, a competent and supportive boss, good pay. You are happy, your husband is happy, and everyone else around you is happy as well, for they no longer need to listen to your tales of woe. Then, a mere six months into the job, the company you work for goes through a reorganization — and your perfect position and your ideal boss are gone. Once again, you're miserable, at the mercy of the changing world around you, and once again you begin your attempts to maneuver yourself into an improved situation, one that will bring you the happiness you continue to long for but never manage to get for too long.

Much of our never-ending dissatisfaction can be traced to our excessive preoccupation with our body, our senses, and our expectation of how the world should be. All our efforts and ingenuity are spent in creating more and more avenues for enjoyment. Yet even so-called successful people, who according to all material standards have achieved a high standard of living, often lead lives of unhappiness, anxiety, and tension. The newspapers are filled with accounts of successful business people and wealthy show-business celebrities mired in lives filled with depression, illegal drugs, broken marriages, and pain.

Thus, at both the individual as well as the community and global levels, happiness is the goal of all of our efforts in life. It is therefore of paramount importance to find out exactly **where happiness is located.** We generally believe that the joy we experience through our sense organs lies *in* the sense objects our sense organs pursue; for example:

- In beautiful music for our ears
- In soothing creams for our skin
- In exciting shapes for our eyes

As we pursue this belief, we constantly try to get more and more of the objects that our sense organs crave. Many of us succeed in gathering a great amount of pleasing objects — but in time we find that our happiness is not at all greater than before: It did not grow in proportion to the wealth we gathered around us.

Wealth is by no means a measure of happiness, since joy is not to be found in the sense objects. If it were contained in those objects, each object would provide the same amount of joy to all those who came in contact with it. But this is not the case:

> A man smoking a cigar after a satisfying meal in a fancy restaurant is overwhelmed with pleasure at crowning his feast with such a relaxing, enjoyable activity. However, the

person sitting two tables away is going through agony, because her evening is spoiled by the pungent fumes she loathes.

If joy is not in the sense objects, then where exactly is it located?

This leads to the fundamental question:

What is happiness?

These questions were the basis upon which the ancient masters made thorough investigations into the human personality. They discovered that **happiness is a state of mind:**

- When the mind is agitated, we feel sorrow and anxiety.
- When the mind is tranquil, we feel joy.

Thus, happiness is measured by the tranquillity of our mind. Tranquillity may at times be brought about by contact with sense objects, but that tranquillity turns out to be only temporary. Lasting satisfaction does not come from sense gratification.

We wait for weeks to receive the stereo set that we ordered some time ago, our anticipation growing with each passing day. The set finally arrives. We start playing with its knobs, adjusting the balance and the volume. We spend several hours playing our favorite music. We even show it to our friends: Somehow their reaction doesn't quite measure up to our expectations. We begin to feel a staleness in our joy. Another day passes, and our joy has now truly lost its first glow. Our happiness is no longer as intense as in that first moment of fulfilled anticipation. Soon our usual anxieties have taken possession of the mind — once again.

Because most of us have not analyzed the nature of happiness sufficiently, we continue to believe that sense objects are the source of all happiness. The masses run after the material world in vain. The spiritual masters of all ages have asserted that the human being has the unique capacity to quiet the mind and thus learn to enjoy real tranquillity — without having to depend helplessly upon any object or thing. This capacity lies dormant in all of us.

The Happiness Equation

The scriptures explain this truth and help to awaken the dormant faculty in us. Once we learn the art of quieting the mind, our mind will no longer find it necessary to pursue the objects of the world for gaining peace and happiness. At that point we will have learned the real joy of living. We will get established in a state of permanent happiness, independent of the environment or the circumstances. A person who has achieved this state stands out like a beacon-light for others.

Happiness can be expressed in the form of an equation, as follows:

$$\text{Happiness} = \frac{\text{Number of desires fulfilled}}{\text{Number of desires entertained}}$$

We can increase the amount of happiness by either of the following:

1. Increasing the numerator
2. Decreasing the denominator

Fulfillment of existing desires quiets the agitations created by desires. Again, if we have fewer desires, the agitations in the mind are lessened. In either case, it is the lessening of agitations that quiets the mind and therefore produces happiness.

The formula works. However, there is one caution about working on the numerator only: Fulfilling our desires generally causes more desires to spring up.

No sooner do we have the desire for a new house fulfilled, then springs up the desire for new carpeting. As soon as the house is freshly recarpeted, a previously unknown desire for a deck looms its head. No sooner is the deck finished, then the desire for a swimming pool has us in its grips. It never stops.

And as the number of desires increases, the denominator increases, resulting in reduced happiness. Thus, the best way of establishing permanent happiness is to reduce the number of desires entertained by directing our thoughts to a higher ideal of principle.

For Your Study and Reflection

2. Happiness

STUDY QUESTIONS, Level 1

1. Recall and describe a time in your life when a certain desire goaded you to action. Trace the sequence of events in your mind: desire, anticipation, fulfillment, aftermath. How did you feel three days after your desire was fulfilled? three weeks afterward? three months afterward?

2. How would you characterize your thoughts when you are feeling anxious? Do you have few or many thoughts at that time?

STUDY QUESTIONS, Level 2

1. Do you think that society should be concerned that too many people might choose to renounce their desires to gain a calm mind? Do you think it would slow down the pace of progress? Why or why not?

2. Why do the scriptures describe our attachment to sense objects as a form of bondage?

FOR YOUR REFLECTION

- He who has liberated himself from the terrible bonds of desires for sense objects (which are very difficult to renounce) is alone fit for liberation; none else, even if he is well versed in all the six schools of philosophy. (Shankaracharya, *Vivekacūḍāmaṇi 78*)

- As fire is enveloped by smoke, as a mirror by dust, as a fetus by the womb, so this [wisdom] is enveloped by that [desire]. (*Bhagavad Gītā* III:38)

- He attains peace into whom all desires enter as waters enter the ocean, which, filled from all sides, remains unmoved . . . . (*Bhagavad Gītā* II:70)

FURTHER READING

- Shankaracharya, *Vivekachoodamani (Vivekacūḍāmaṇi)*. Commentary by Swami Chinmayananda. Bombay, India: Central Chinmaya Mission Trust, 1987. Verses 76-82.

Religion 3

You are destined to be great. So is everyone else on this planet. Success should be your habit.

Yet, millions of people in the world are suffering. They live disorganized lives; they suffer the agony of failure.

If we look around us, we see that for every happy and successful person, there are hundreds who are disappointed and unhappy. People manage to get themselves crushed in the world of material competition and the rat race of the work-a-day world.

Innate Perfection

The spiritual literature of the world says: This unhappy state need not be ours. If each individual learns the art of approaching life correctly, everyone can be fully happy and successful. Each one of us is essentially perfect; the possibilities hiding within us are infinitely great. We have within ourselves all the resources, abilities, energy, and power for building up supremely happy and successful lives, not only for ourselves, but for others around us also.

We all possess this one great gift — the ability to discover and develop the infinite possibilities within us.

If we organize our life in such a way so as to discover the great potential within us, and if we order our behavior so as to nurture and nourish that potential, our life will be well spent. Our success lies in the amount of transformation we can bring about in our character and behavior. The question is not how many talents each one of us has, but how much of our existing talents we explore and develop. An individual can have many talents — yet can be a miserable failure in life. The successful person is one who makes practical use of at least one great talent that he or she possesses.

Our present and future societies therefore depend on what you and I do. Never look outside yourself for help. Don't fall into the delusion that the influence of others will enable you to do better and accomplish more. Although others can inspire you to action, your success depends on yourself alone.

What we regularly encourage and cultivate in our minds determines our character and ultimately our destiny. An intelligent choice of thoughts can transform our character as well as our lives. Thus, the entire destiny of our lives lies in our own hands. We can rebuild our own future.[1]

Knowledge — the Secret Strength

Religion is not for animals; the tigers and the bears have no religion.

Religion is the remedy for a particular unrest felt by the human being, even when he or she has all the best that life has to offer. Religion is the technique by which we get our minds and intellects trained to grasp and understand the larger themes of the universe and our own place in it.

This science of the spirit has a very practical use for us. I am not talking of the religion of bell ringing or light showing or incense burning. I am talking of an approach to life that helps us to discover a new strength to face the challenges of life and a new courage of conviction to live honestly serving others. That which provides us with such a method for masterly living is true religion.

Religion does not attempt to improve the condition of the world. It does not aim to help us gain freedom from all needs and thus grant us a higher standard of living. Instead, it teaches us a method for creating in ourselves the equipoise

[1] See Chapter 10, "Karma," for a full discussion of this topic.

to stand up to life's situations, meeting efficiently the ever-changing world of challenges. True religion imparts to us **the art of living.**

Scientists have learned to understand increasingly more about the secrets of Nature. The results of their research have given to the age more strength, daring, and vitality. Science has conquered Nature, and humankind, as a result of the knowledge it has accumulated, has gained mastery over the outer world. The secret of our strength is knowledge.

Yet, despite our mastery over the outer world, we still feel unhappy and unfulfilled. The great sages of the past taught that a particular kind of knowledge can transform our lives and bring to us a fullness of satisfaction that no other endeavor yields: knowledge of our inner spiritual constitution, a knowledge that gives us mastery over our lives.

The knowledge of which the sages spoke grew out of their analysis of human beings and their contacts with the outer world. They defined the instruments that contact the world and that experience life as the body, the mind, and the intellect. Then they determined how these instruments can best be readjusted so as to bring forth greater success and happiness in our lives. This analysis is the content of all sacred textbooks, whether they belong to the traditions of Christianity, Hinduism, Judaism, Islam, Buddhism, or any other major religious persuasion.

Religion begins as a scientific reevaluation of life. Just as the material scientists retire to their laboratories to do their research, the spiritual masters have retired to the cool and silent valleys of the Himalayas or to the deserts of the Middle East to do their research on the human personality. While material scientists take the outer world as their field of investigation, the subjective scientists take their own inner world of experiences as the field of their search for truth.

- Scientists try to understand "What is the world?"
- Spiritual masters seek to discover "Who or what is the human being?"

True philosophy and science are based on life's experiences. The philosophy of the Hindus has emphasized the importance of experience more than the philosophy of the West. And in Hindu philosophy, Vedanta has the unique distinction of having based itself on the entire range of human experience — namely, the three states of waking, dream, and deep sleep.[2]

An experience can be one's own or that of another who is a reliable authority. Let us consider modern scientific research as an example. How does scientific research proceed? Science is based on innumerable hypotheses that provide possible explanations of certain natural phenomena. As new data accumulate, the laws and theories of science may need revision. Thus, science is a growing tradition, the present research being performed on the basis of the truthfulness of past conclusions.

The scriptures represent the data gathered and conclusions arrived at by generations of sages, the scientists of the spirit. Their theories and conclusions have been confirmed as true by at least a hundred mystics in every century all over the world for many thousands of years.

Religion is the technique of perfect living, of gaining better mastery over ourselves. It is the process by which we can bring forth an effective personality out of even a person shattered by disappointments.

> The transformation of Arjuna, whose dialogue with Lord Krishna constitutes the eighteen chapters of the *Bhagavad Gītā*, Hinduism's best-known scripture, is an example of how spiritual wisdom can transform one's life. Krishna's eighteen discourses cured Arjuna's life-crippling despondency and transformed him into a dynamic warrior anchored in the spirit.

[2] See Chapter 14, "Three Worlds," for a full discussion of this topic.

For Your Study and Reflection

3. Religion

STUDY QUESTIONS, Level 1

1. What does religion mean to you? What do you think is the main goal of religion?

2. How do you think religion can have practical value in your life?

3. How can depending on the good influence of others help you? How can it hinder you?

STUDY QUESTIONS, Level 2

1. What do you think is the nature of the "unrest" that human beings feel when they strive for something more than the material life?

2. How can the nature of our thinking determine our destiny? Provide some examples.

3. Explain how knowledge is our secret strength in transforming our lives.

FOR YOUR REFLECTION

- The art of spiritual living is subtler than all other arts, more demanding than all known sciences, more precise than literature, more adventurous than space-walking. (Swami Chinmayananda, *We Must*, page 56)

- The more we move toward Him, the Infinite and the Omnipotent dwelling ever in our hearts, the more we shall realize that we have unlimited resources. We must.

  The more we add to our self-confidence, the more we bring out our courage, the more we discover new efficiencies in us, the more we get sustained by faith in ourselves. We Must. (Swami Chinmayananda, *We Must*, pages 18-19)

FURTHER READING

- *The Holy Geeta* (*Bhagavad Gītā*). Commentary by Swami Chinmayananda. Bombay, India: Central Chinmaya Mission Trust, 1980. Chapter II.

- Swami Chinmayananda, *We Must*. Napa, California: Chinmaya Publications West, 1976. Chapters 5-6.

Balance 4

When we contact the world of objects, we experience either joy or sorrow. A series of such experiences constitutes life.

The material scientists — those who investigate the economic, political, and scientific fields — have always believed that life could be made happier by improving the objects and situations in the world. With this idea in mind, they have put forth great efforts for many hundreds of years to create the present world of achievements. Today, we live in considerable comfort. Yet, we feel ever-increasing stress in life and little lasting happiness.

The Sacred and the Secular

When our control on outer nature far exceeds our control over our own inner nature, an imbalance is created. This imbalance is at the crux of our problems today.

Philosophy and religion rehabilitate our inner selves and provide us with the equilibrium to make our lives more fulfilling. Without the rehabilitation of the human personality, a mere rearrangement and beautification of the external world is of little help in providing peace and happiness. To do so is as absurd as putting a sumptuous meal in front of a person suffering from indigestion, with little taste for food.

Material growth raises the **standard of living,** whereas spiritual, inner rehabilitation improves the **standard of life.** Both the standard of living and the standard of life have to be equally developed in order for us to go through life with ease and cheer.

> The standard of living is like the mast of a ship; if we want it to be high, the keel must be made deep to balance the height. The depth of the keel measures the standard of life. When the mast is out of proportion, the vessel topples over. If the keel is sufficiently deep and broad, the ship is stable regardless of the height of the mast.

So too in life: If the standard of living alone is raised at the expense of the standard of life, the society slides downhill. Whenever the standard of life is well established, the society grows peaceful and wholesome.

In addition to the objective scientists (such as the economists, politicians, and scientists), another category of scientist exists: the subjective scientist. He investigates the human personality and draws our attention to the divine center within each of us. Whereas the objective scientists strive to raise the standard of living, the subjective scientists' efforts are directed at raising the standard of life.

Scientific achievements have a worthy place in human society. It is only fanatic materialism and secularism, divorced from inner development, that is bad for us. Similarly, a fanatically religious approach, without material development, can lead us into a dark age — as we experienced in the Middle Ages of Europe. The obvious solution is a harmonious blending of the sacred and the secular.

The Dual Path

Material prosperity, by itself, cannot give us happiness — if we have not developed a healthy inner personality.

In the first stages of inner growth we gain added fulfillment by practicing intelligent self-restraint, as the scriptural teachings of the world tell us. We generally don't like the idea of self-control or discipline. The typical individual today considers discipline as a shackle on his freedom, so he avoids spiritual practices. Then there are others who unintelligently follow the letter of the scriptures and forcibly deny themselves all enjoyments. When a person practices such unintelligent self-denial, he creates for himself mental suppressions.

If, with the help of the world's scriptures, we gain an intelligent understanding of the laws governing our personality, we will find our lives inspired with a nobler vision of life. As we progress in our inward expansion, our baser tendencies drop off. This rejection of baser values, following an understanding of a higher vision, is sublimation (as opposed to suppression).

> **Suppression** results from a forceful self-denial based on either blind belief, unrestrained enthusiasm, or sheer superstition. Suppression leads to the degeneration of our inner selves.
>
> **Sublimation** is the elimination of some of our false values as a result of intellectual conviction. As we learn to understand the higher values of life, our mental vision broadens, and the lower tendencies automatically disappear. Sublimation strengthens our inner selves.

Our personality is clogged with imperfections, just as a mass of cotton is mixed with impurities:

> To remove the impurities from cotton, the cotton is carded: The cotton mass is combed and beaten so that the pure cotton separates from the heavier impurities. Similarly, to remove our negative tendencies, we learn the nobler values in life. As we assimilate them, our minds soar to higher realms of thought, leaving our negativities behind.

The basic knowledge of what is good and what is bad is known to us all. In spite of it, however, we often choose a path that is not beneficial to our well-being. The Vedantic masters analyzed the reason for such conduct and discovered that there are two distinct paths in life:

- The path of the pleasant (*preyas*)
- The path of the good (*śreyas*)

We are confronted with choosing one of the two paths at every single moment of our lives. The path of the pleasant, as the name suggests, pleases, fascinates, and entices us to take it — now! In contrast, the path of the good may have some unpleasant aspects at first. The path of the pleasant provides immediate pleasure, but later ends up in disappointment and sorrow. The path of the good can be unpleasant at first, but later brings happiness and fulfillment.

The Path of the Pleasant	*The Path of the Good*
• Guided by the demands of the sense organs	• Guided by the subtle intellect
• Temporary joy in the beginning, but sorrow later	• Unpleasant in the beginning, but provides permanent happiness later
• More alluring; caters to the extroverted mind	• Has a hidden beauty, perceived by the introverted mind only
• The path of devolution	• The path of evolution
• The path for the majority of people	• The path followed by only a few people
• Based on sense gratification	• Based on sound knowledge
• Denounced by all religions	• Recommended by all religions

Every action of each living being is motivated by an irresistible instinct to be happy. Happiness seems to be the goal of every struggle and strife in life. Even a worm crawling in refuse wanders about motivated by a hope that it will reach a greater joy. Only in full and absolute contentment all searching will end, and this supreme state of happiness is the goal of all life and the subject of all the scriptures of the world.

It is in this light that the rishis classified all actions into the two categories, that is, with reference to their results. The fruits of action can be of two kinds:

1. Those contributing to the ephemeral joys in life
2. Those leading to immortal bliss

That is, our efforts can either contribute to some immediate passing material gain, or they can contribute in the long run to our self-nurturing and self-purification.

> A corrupt official, through foul and fiendish methods, can excel in accumulating wealth. To the ignorant and sensuous this may appear as an inviting prospect and a welcome success. On the other hand, each of us has the choice to build our lives upon more enduring principles of life such as honesty, piety, mercy, love, and tolerance, and to live for the greater wealth of inner peace and joy.

The weak-minded try to gain immediate flickers of joy by choosing the path of the pleasant, and thus deny themselves the chance to enjoy more lasting happiness later. People of inner strength choose the path of the good, unmindful of any unpleasantness and material privations, ready to suffer in the course of their higher pursuits. They are the ones who emerge as mighty personalities who not only lead fulfilling lives themselves, but also inspire the rest of society toward a more peaceful and happy life.

For Your Study and Reflection

4. Balance

STUDY QUESTIONS, Level 1

1. Give three examples of following the path of the pleasant and three examples of following the path of the good.

2. What is the main motivation behind our actions? How does this motivation lead us to choose either the path of the pleasant or the path of the good?

3. In your own words, describe what is meant by the "standard of life." Contrast it with the "standard of living."

STUDY QUESTIONS, Level 2

1. Explain how sublimation can elevate our lives and how suppression can become a destructive force in our personality.

2. Give some examples from daily life of how sublimation can be put into practice.

3. Why does the path of the pleasant have so much allure for us?

FOR YOUR REFLECTION

- One is good, while the other is pleasant. These two, having different objectives, chain a man. Blessed is he who, between them, chooses the good alone; but he who chooses what is pleasant loses the true end. (*Kaṭha Upaniṣad* I:II:1)

- Both the good and the pleasant approach the mortal; the intelligent man examines and distinguishes between them; the intelligent man prefers the good to the pleasant. The ignorant man chooses "for getting and keeping" the pleasant for the sake of his body. (*Kaṭha Upaniṣad* I:II:2)

- Know that mortality soon overtakes a foolish man who walks the dangerous path of sense pleasures. Whereas one who sticks to the path of divinity, according to the instructions of well-meaning and noble gurus, constantly walks the path divine, helped by his own reasoning faculty. He achieves the end; know for certain that this is true. (Shankaracharya, *Vivekacūḍāmaṇi* 81)

FURTHER READING

- *Katha Upanishad (Kaṭha Upaniṣad)*. Commentary by Swami Chinmayananda. Bombay, India: Central Chinmaya Mission Trust, 1989. Section I:II.

BMI 5

Religion attempts to bring about a transformation in our inner lives. It teaches us how to master ourselves, to forge an unshakeable tranquillity, and to live lives of inspired joy, irrespective of outer circumstances. This is the theme of all the scriptures of the world.

The Equipment of Experience

With this theme in mind, the ancient masters examined life. They saw that life is a series of experiences and that any definition of life must necessarily accept our moment-to-moment experiences as the units of life, just as each brick is a unit of a wall. The strength or weakness of a wall depends upon the quality and texture of the bricks that comprise it. Similarly, the types of experiences we have in life determine the nature of our life.

We gain an experience when we receive and respond to a stimulus from the world. An experience is not possible without three fundamental factors:

1. The experiencer
2. The object of experience
3. The relationship between the two, the experiencing

These three factors are essential for gaining any experience.

> Mira (subject) receives a cable (object) containing the tragic news of the death of her grandmother but does not read the contents of it. In this case, although the subject and the object are present, no experience of sorrow results since the subject and object are not yet connected. If, however, a relationship between the subject and object is established by Mira's reading the contents of the cable, the third aspect, experiencing, becomes the connecting link to complete the experience.

The experiencer is the subject who gains experiences of the world through the instruments of experience, which are the body, the mind, and the intellect. Everyone of us gains experiences of three different worlds through these three different kinds of equipment. The three worlds are the fields of our experience:

1. Through the body, we experience **the world of objects**
2. Through the mind, we experience **the world of emotions**
3. Through the intellect, we experience **the world of thoughts**

If a person can experience the world of objects through her body, then she must be different from her body. If she experiences the world of feelings through her mind, then she, the experiencer, cannot be the mind. Again, if she gains experiences of the world of ideas through the intellect, she cannot be the intellect. She seems to be a different factor altogether from these three instruments of experience, though she does have a very intimate relationship with them.

The subject, identified with each of three instruments, becomes a different aspect of personality:

1. Identified with the body, she becomes the **perceiver**, experiencing the world of objects.
2. Identified with the mind, she becomes the **feeler**, experiencing the world of emotions.

3. Identified with the intellect, she becomes the **thinker**, experiencing the world of thoughts (ideas).

However, she, the subject, is neither the fields of experience (objects-emotions-thoughts, or OET), nor the instruments of experience (body-mind-intellect, or BMI). She must be totally different from them.

The Supreme Reality

That principle by whose mere presence the intellect thinks, the mind feels, and the body perceives is the supreme Reality (*Brahman*), the substratum for all experiences of the body, mind, and intellect. This principle that lends its light to every being is, according to Vedanta, the divine principle *Om* — also known as the Self (*Ātman*), pure Consciousness, or pure Awareness. That by which I gain my experiences, you gain your experiences, and he and she gain their experiences is one and the same.

> Electrical energy running through various pieces of electrical equipment and expressing itself differently in them is one and the same everywhere, at all times. The heater, the bulb, the radio are all different types of equipment, but they express themselves because of one vitality alone — electricity.

The divine Principle is one, yet appears as many when It expresses Itself through the varied instruments of body, mind, and intellect. One Principle holds the varied objects of this universe together, as a string holds flowers of different shapes and colors to form one beautiful garland. The plant, the animal, the human kingdoms — all are enlivened by this one Principle, enabling all of them to gain their own particular experiences.

The three types of equipment — the body, mind, and intellect, or BMI — constitute the matter envelopments around our inner Self. The mind and intellect are but subtler forms of matter. By itself, BMI is inert and insentient. The divine Principle (the Self, the Spirit) is what animates the equipment and causes it to function. The pure Self, without such equipment, has no expression of Its own. It is the marriage of the two — of Spirit (*Puruṣa*) with matter (*prakṛti*) — that enables the manifestation of life as birth, activity, and growth.

Let's return to the analogy of electricity:

> An electrical bulb, by itself, has no expression of light. Electricity, by itself, has no expression.
>
> When electricity comes in contact with a light bulb, electricity expresses itself as light.

Similarly,

> The body-mind-intellect equipment is inert.
>
> The pure Self, by Itself, has no expression.
>
> When the Self pulsates through the body-mind-intellect, the pure Self becomes manifest as life.

Pure Consciousness, the Self, is also referred to as the changeless Substratum upon which all changes take place. The body and its perceptions are constantly changing. So are the mind and its emotions and the intellect and its thoughts. We can notice these changes occurring in our equipment. But recognition of change is possible only with reference to a changeless entity.

> Two persons sitting in a closed compartment of a moving train do not observe any change with respect to each other. However, when they look out the window, they can notice the movement of the train with reference to the stationary objects along the tracks.

The fact that we recognize the changes occurring in us establishes the existence of a changeless entity. This changeless entity is the pure Self. We can summarize the nature of the Self as follows:

- The Self, by Itself, has no expression.
- The Self is the Life Principle that enlivens matter.
- The Self is something other than the body-mind-intellect equipment.
- The Self is the changeless Reality that enables us to recognize the changes that occur at our physical, mental, and intellectual levels.

That changeless Reality is known by many names, several of which will be used throughout this book:

- The Absolute
- *Ātman* (the Self), the immanent (microcosmic) aspect of *Brahman*, the supreme Reality
- *Brahman*, the supreme Reality in its transcendent (macrocosmic) aspect
- The Life Principle
- *Om*
- Pure Awareness
- Pure Consciousness
- The Self (*Ātman*); the supreme Self; the pure Self
- Spirit
- The supreme Reality (*Brahman*)
- Truth

A Sanskrit term used to describe the supreme Reality is *sat-cit-ānanda,* which means "existence-knowledge-bliss." *Sat* is that which remains unchanged in all the three periods of time; that is, in the past, the present, and the future.

An analogy that explains *sat* relates the reality of clay to the reality of the jug made of clay. The *sat* aspect of the jug is clay,

> which existed before the jug was fashioned, which exists now in the form of a jug, and which will remain after the jug is destroyed. Like the clay jug, everything perishable is made of a substance that is fundamental and permanent.

The fundamental substance of which the perishable world is made is *Brahman*, the supreme Reality, which was, is, and will remain whether or not the world exists. *Brahman* looked at from the standpoint of existence and nonexistence is *sat*, existence at all times. *Brahman* is never nonexistent.

Cit is pure Awareness or Consciousness. After learning that *Brahman* is ever existent (*sat*), we must ask if *Brahman* is sentient or insentient. The word *cit* reveals that *Brahman* is, indeed, Consciousness or Awareness Itself. This Consciousness exists in all states of experience — waking, dream, and deep sleep — illumining everything experienced. In deep sleep, It even illumines no-thing.

We may conclude that *Brahman* is existence (*sat*) and Consciousness (*cit*), but still we may ask if this existent Consciousness is of the nature of happiness or sorrow. The word *ānanda* speaks to this question by revealing that the nature of *Brahman* is, indeed, bliss, fullness, and joy. *Ānanda*, or bliss, is the experience gained when you are with yourself.

> For example, when you desire an object and then that desire is fulfilled, the momentary happiness is that of being with yourself: At that moment you are totally satisfied with yourself and do not want to be something else or have something else. The state then experienced is called *ānanda*, which is the fundamental nature of all human beings.

An object may appear to produce happiness for a short while, but the object is only an instrument. As we have already seen,[1] an object, by itself, does not possess the faculty of happiness or sorrow, because the same object has different appeal to different people, or different appeal to the same

[1] In Chapter 2, "Happiness."

person at different times. The locus of happiness is ourselves. Therefore, to find happiness, we need not search far and wide, as any searching outside ourselves would only take us further away from the locus of happiness, ourselves. We need only realize our true nature, which is existence-knowledge-bliss.

Heat and cold are the perceptions of the body, happiness and sorrow are feelings of the mind, right and wrong are the conceptual judgments of the intellect. But when you are one with the Self, which lends life to all these kinds of equipment, you are not tainted by any of the experiences gained by them. Rooted in the Self, you experience the divinity that is present everywhere and at all times, one without a second.

We find that the world of objects (OET) plays out its follies according to a law over which we have little control. But we do have control over our reactions to our experiences in that world. Objects must come in contact with our minds in order to produce a reaction in them. If we can train our minds so that they react positively to any object under any circumstances, all our reactions will be positive. Happiness and peace are his who has trained his mind to react positively to the outer world at all times. Once we have mental equipment that keeps a steady poise and balance under all circumstances, even if the outer world remains full of imperfections and sorrows, we shall have an unbroken experience of full contentment.

We never recognize and experience the outer world as it is, but only as our mind and intellect interpret it.

> The wearer of a pair of blue-tinted goggles sees the world as blue. Similarly, we experience the world according to the constitution of our minds: sad mind, sad world; happy mind, happy world; agitated mind, agitated world.[2]

---

[2] You will read more about the characteristics of the mind-intellect equipment in Chapter 9, "Mind."

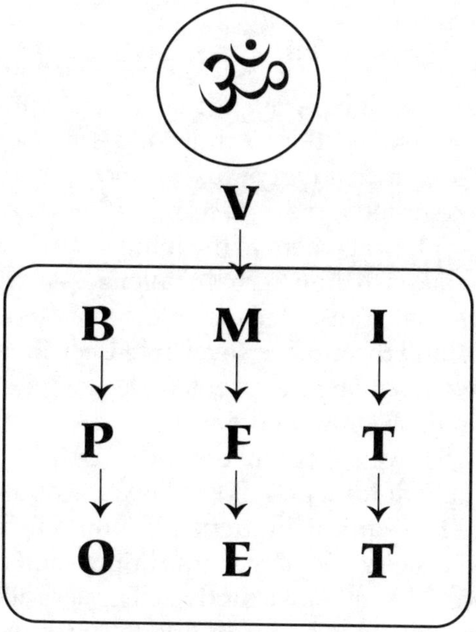

Through
the BODY (**B**), MIND (**M**), INTELLECT (**I**),
the PERCEIVER (**P**), FEELER (**F**), THINKER (**T**)
becomes enmeshed in the world of
OBJECTS (**O**), EMOTIONS (**E**), and THOUGHTS (**T**).

But when we transcend our
VĀSANĀS (**V**),
we realize our true Self,
OM,
the supreme Reality.

Vāsanās

For it to come to the right decision, the intellect must have the correct data. However, the reading of a situation is often distorted by our unsteady, confused, and sometimes even severely disintegrated mind. The mind gathers the reports of our senses and presents them to the intellect to decide on the response to be taken to the external challenge. When the mind is unsteady, the data presented become a confused, misinterpreted jumble; and the intellect, even if its decisions are right, is not effective in solving the problem, as its decisions have been based on misrepresented data.

We are what we are because of the calibre of our mental and intellectual equipment. And the texture and quality of the mind-intellect equipment depend upon our innate tendencies called *vāsanās*. *Vāsanās* are the impressions left in our mind when we act with selfish motives. The very ability of the intellect to think and to judge is conditioned by the unmanifest factor in us called *vāsanās*, which in modern psychological parlance is known as the unconscious. This unconscious mass or tendencies, inclinations, and urges is composed of impressions the personality has gathered from its own thoughts and actions in the past.

> If I am a drunkard, I have drink-*vāsanās*, and so when I see a bottle of whisky, my reaction is to grab it immediately; whereas you, a perfect teetotaler, will avert your face and walk away in disgust.
>
> If I am a musician, I have music-*vāsanās*, and I take every opportunity to meet with other lovers of music to play, sing, and improvise together.

The *vāsanās* gathered from our past march out into their expression in this sequence:

1. First, as a desiring thought in the intellect, a scheme that the intellect devises for winning more happiness
2. Then, as an emotional thought in the mind, an agitation

that disturbs the thought flow as the mind begins to grapple with the desire

3. Last, as an act at the body level, the final expression of the erstwhile, unmanifest *vāsanā*

Each one of us is thus a helpless expression of our past, recorded in us as our *vāsanās*. Every action of ours is the fulfillment of a desire, which in turn is the gross manifestation of a *vāsanās*. Our *vāsanās*, then, become the prime movers of all of our desires and consequent actions. As long as we have *vāsanās*, desires will keep gurgling up in us, resulting in mental agitations that lead us to the expression of those desires in action.

In Sanskrit, the word *vāsanā* means "fragrance." Each one of us has *vāsanās* peculiar to us; each one of us has a particular "personality fragrance" defined by our *vāsanās*. In other words, an individual is nothing but a manifest form of his or her unmanifest urges. The differences between individuals are caused by the differences in their *vāsanā*-patterns.

> Desires, thoughts, and actions spring forth from our *vāsanās* just as sound emanates from the grooves cut in a phonograph record. Depending on the grooves in the record, the sound that pours forth is sweet or harsh, fast or slow in its beat. Similarly, if our *vāsanās* are noble, our actions are also noble. If our *vāsanās* are coarse, our actions are likewise coarse.

Vāsanās can be classified under three categories:

- Social urges *(loka vāsanās)*. These tendencies urge us to follow the patterns of our time.
- Physical urges *(deha vāsanās)*. These urges render us slaves to our physical body.
- The urge to know *(śāstra vāsanās)*. These tendencies lead us to mere scholarly study of various kinds of knowledge, either religious or secular.

Just as our individual *vāsanās* define our individual personality, so also the combined *vāsanās* of the individuals in a community define the community, and likewise the combined *vāsanās* of the people in a nation or even the entire world define the nation and the world. Thus, national problems are essentially eruptions caused by the *vāsanās* in all the individuals in the nation put together. Therefore, the scriptures declare: Only through individual perfection can world perfection be achieved.

Beyond BMI

The three conditionings on the pure Self — the body, mind, and intellect — must be transcended in order for us to regain our original nature, the limitless, blissful nature of *Om*. We cannot do this by merely suppressing the equipment, since the cause which produces them, namely, the *vāsanās*, can never be annihilated by destroying its effects. As long as the *vāsanās* are powerful, our equipment will assert itself time and again, even if we succeed in suppressing it for a while. The only method for regaining one's true nature as the pure Self is vigilantly and ceaselessly to divert one's mind and intellect away from preoccupation with the world of objects-emotions-thoughts, toward an awareness of the Self.

We must learn to lift ourselves by ourselves — by our own bootstraps — out of our lower impulses. When we identify ourselves with the Higher in us, the lower automatically drops away. This is true renunciation (*sannyāsa*).

> When Baby Julia matures into a young teenager called Ms. Julia, she no longer longs for the dolls of her childhood. As a child, she clung to her chest full of dolls of various shapes and sizes and coveted the dolls of her neighborhood playmates. However, now with her sights on more mature goals, her desire for playing with dolls has effortlessly dropped away.

When we succeed in identifying ourselves with the Higher in us, all our intellectual restlessness, emotional cravings, and physical appetites wither and fall away, just as the petals of a flower fall to the ground as the fruit emerges.

Vāsanās veil the divinity in us, and therefore they are known as ignorance (*avidyā*). The pure, divine Self is our true nature, but due to our *vāsanās* and consequent agitations of the mind, we become ignorant of our true nature and identify ourselves with the personality and its limitations.

All thoughts such as "I am the body," "I am the mind," and "I am the intellect" arise from our ignorance of the supreme Reality, *Om*. Ignorance of our true nature makes us feel a sense of imperfection in ourselves, and we try to make up for this sense of limitation by creating desires to be fulfilled in the mistaken notion that their fulfillment will bring us closer to a sense of perfection, a feeling of completeness.

A Self-realized person is one who has destroyed ignorance by his direct, personal experience of the Self. This does not mean that somehow we need to *make* the Self shine forth — just as we need not make the sun shine by any means whatsoever. The sun is ever bright, illumining the world throughout the four seasons. Only the passing clouds hide its glory. As the clouds pass away, the sun behind them is revealed. Similarly, the Self is ever present everywhere. It illumines every object and experience and makes Its presence known by Its life-giving powers. Once the veil of ignorance (mass of *vāsanās*) is removed, the real nature of the Self is revealed in Its resplendent glory.

An individual is the Self *as though* contaminated by ignorance, which finds expression in the world as thoughts and actions. The Self thus conditioned by the body-mind-intellect (BMI) is the individuality (*jīva*), or ego, otherwise known as the perceiver-feeler-thinker (PFT). This individuality is the one who suffers the limitations of matter. The *jīva* can be compared to the reflection we see in a mirror:

> If the reflecting surface of a mirror is imperfect, we may look distorted, yet we know that the distortion is not our true

identity. The ugliness of our reflection can end only when the reflecting surface is either cleaned or straightened.

Similarly, the reflecting surface of the mind allows the light of the pure Self to shine through only if our mental equipment has become steady and pure. In fact, an absolutely purified and steadied mind is no more a mind, since a mind is nothing but thoughts in motion. When the mind has ended, the ego-center perceived for so long as the individuality rebounds back to its original nature, the Self.

Spiritual unfoldment cannot take place merely because of an intellectual appreciation of how we can achieve Self-realization. Evolution occurs only when a corresponding change in our subjective life takes place. Therefore, active and enthusiastic participation by the seeker in reeducating his thought life will alone lead to success in reaching the goal of realizing the Self.

Learn how to dissolve the *vāsanās* and remove the ignorance that separates you from the effulgent flow of divinity into your life — and you will transcend the body-mind-intellect equipment to realize your true nature, *Om*.

For Your Study and Reflection

5. BMI

STUDY QUESTIONS, Level 1

1. Describe one *vāsanā* that you think has given rise to many of the activities in your life. Give one example of the play of this *vāsanā* in your life. (Example: music-*vāsanā*.)

2. Which three aspects of the personality constitute the ego (*jīva*)?

3. Give three characteristics of the pure Self.

STUDY QUESTIONS, Level 2

1. Describe an experience wherein your particular instrument of experience (body-mind-intellect) perceived an event or an object differently from another person. What particular characteristic of your BMI equipment defined the event or object for you?

2. What do you think is the difference between the immanent aspect of the Godhead (*Ātman,* the Self) and the transcendent aspect of the Godhead (*Brahman,* the supreme Reality)?

3. Why do we say that the Self is "one without a second?"

FOR YOUR REFLECTION

- The soul appears to be finite because of ignorance. When ignorance is destroyed, the Self, which does not admit of any multiplicity, reveals Itself by Itself, like the sun when the clouds pass away. (Shankaracharya, *Ātma Bodha* 4)

- Just as a lamp illumines a jar or a pot, so also the *Ātman* illumines the mind, the sense organs, etc. These material objects, by themselves, cannot illumine themselves, because they are inert. (Shankaracharya, *Ātma Bodha* 28)

- *Ātman* is an ever-present Reality. Yet, because of ignorance, It is not realized. On the destruction of ignorance, *Ātman* is realized. It is like the missing ornament on one's neck. (Shankaracharya, *Ātma Bodha* 44)

FURTHER READING

- Shankaracharya, *Ātma Bodha*. Commentary by Swami Chinmayananda. Bombay, India: Central Chinmaya Mission Trust, 1987.

Action 6

You and I are alive. Therefore, we cannot but be engaged in action. As long as we live, we have to act, for life pulsating through the body becomes activity in the outer world. Life expresses itself in action, as death does in inaction. But actions vary from person to person.

> A farmer working in the fields sweats with exertion. A poet in the midst of his greatest creation doesn't seem to be working at all from the farmer's point of view. From the standpoint of a poet, a scientist is wasting public money. From the scientist's standpoint, an ordinary thinker is wasting his time. From all their points of view, Buddha sitting under a tree in meditation is an idler, an unnecessary leach upon society.

In every case, each person may say to the other that he is an idler, but each one knows how vigorously he himself is working.

> A great painter was once sitting near a wayside pool, throwing stones into the water and watching the play of light and shade upon the ripples. An ordinary man, walking along the road, carrying milk to the nearby town to sell, jealously looked at the man and thought, "This fool is sitting idly from morning to evening, eating food that is brought to him. How unfair! I have already put in eight hours of work, and I cannot make both ends meet. What an injustice!"
>
> The simple villager did not know that the person against whom he had complained was no less an artist than

Michelangelo, the great painter, who as a result of observing the ripples, reproduced them on canvas. Michelangelo wanted to observe the play of light and shade on the ripples so that he could capture their alluring beauty in a painting.

Michelangelo was vigorously studying, but others thought he was idling away his time. It is that man, the so-called idler, who produced the immortal paintings and sculptures we all know, while the milkman who was supposed to have toiled so honestly for society died like a bug, leaving nothing for posterity.

Everyone must work, but what matters is how we work — what is the quality of the activity we are engaged in.

Three Kinds of Action

The great thinkers of India classified all people engaged in activity in three categories:

- Laborers
- Workers
- Persons of achievement

The difference between these people is not in the work they do but the way in which they do *it*. Because their temperaments and mental outlooks differ, their goals in life differ also. Their diverse goals, in turn, affect their activities.

When I say laborer, I am in no way bringing disgrace to ordinary physical labor. I am not using the word in that sense. For the purposes of this discussion, laborer means one who has almost no ideals in life and works selfishly in order to earn money. He uses that money only for himself and his family. Although he may work very hard, he works only for getting more money to make his life more comfortable. His goal in life does not go beyond his own egocentric desires. By this definition of a laborer, a political leader of high stature is a laborer if he puts forth his entire energies with the idea that, as he does so, he will get more income for his personal gain. If you ask such a person why he wants to earn money, he has no motive greater than that he wants to furnish his house beautifully for the sake of his wife and children, for his own pleasure. The person who is self-centered works only for the profit that comes to him. With that profit he does not think of starting a hospital or of establishing an orphanage. A laborer may be a person of high-ranking position, such as a judge, a corporate executive, a scientist, or a writer. As long as he works for his own profit alone, he is a laborer.

A worker is one who works less selfishly and is inspired by a definite ideal in life. The worker doesn't work only for profit, but constantly has a higher ideal in mind as the inspiration for his work. All inspired political, social, and religious leaders are in this category. Every worker has a picture of a perfect society. He struggles hard because he is inspired by a great enthusiasm and a high vision, and he strives to bring that vision into actuality. He wants nothing else from life. He is ready to starve, he is ready to suffer; what he wants in the world is only success for his ideal. In contrast to the laborer, the ego of the worker has been reduced to some degree.

The third variety is very rare. Laborers are many in the world, and workers are fewer in number. But the third variety, called persons of achievement, are very few indeed. It is these people who uplift an entire generation to a higher dignity of morality, a greater virtue in living. Such mighty people are called saints, seers, or prophets. They are incarnations of great virtues and values. They live an ideal life, inspiring others even after their death. The fragrance of their thought and the might and glory of their ideals gather a new momentum as the years pass by. Christ died two thousand years ago, and yet we find that His glory becomes more and more compelling as time passes. In such a person, the ego is totally eliminated, and the person works only for the good of others.

One may ask the person of achievement: "What is it that

you want in the world; why are you working? — O Buddha, why did you work? O Christ, why did you work? O Mohammed, why did you move from place to place, preaching against many odds?" Men of achievement work in the world not for profit, nor for success, but from a feeling that they are doing the right thing, irrespective of whether or not they will be recognized in their lifetime. All that such people want is the secret joy, the sense of fulfillment that they have done the best they could. They do not care whether others recognize them or not, and they remain untouched by either praise or blame.

More often than not, such great persons of achievement are persecuted by society, for they are too idealistic for their age. Against all such obstacles, they live on, inspiring others by their joyous way of life, thus bringing about a new movement of moral change in the society. In time, the morality, the culture, and the civilization of the society they lived in rises to new glory as a result of their work.

All activities can be said to fall into two broad categories:

- Activities motivated by desire
- Activities not motivated by desire

In the first category, the desires motivating a person's actions may be either totally selfish (laborer) or directed to a higher cause such as the welfare of a nation (worker). In the second category, however, no desires at all motivate the person's actions (person of achievement); he does not work in order to gain a given result. The person of achievement is tuned in to the supreme Reality and is always in a state of total fulfillment. He wants nothing, and none of his actions brings him more satisfaction than he already has. An action done without selfish desires *(niṣkāma karma)* is the noblest of all.

The trend of the modern individual is to "look out for number one" (that is, for himself alone). He lacks a vision or an ideal toward which to strive. As a result, there is little enthusiasm or inspiration in his work. Such a person needs to develop an ideal for himself, a purpose larger than just satisfying his senses.

Once we set an ideal for ourselves, joy enters our activities. We develop a keen appetite for life. We can thus raise the mind from the attitude of a laborer to the dignity of a worker. Then, if we work less and less selfishly until we discover fulfillment in the act of work itself, we reach the state of a person of achievement.

The Secret of Success

The value of work is measured by the idea that inspires us to do it. The quality of action improves as we adopt higher ideals to inspire our work. The nobler the ideal, the greater will be the beauty of our action. All great contributors to society have had such ideals, and their actions have left behind rich achievements for many generations to enjoy.

Many people today don't have a definite ideal to channel their activities. Many work with a selfish attitude and with a vision that does not go beyond the interests of their own families. When we work with a narrow, selfish attitude, we find little joy in the work, only monotony and fatigue.

Fatigue in work results mainly from mental dissipation. Often a comfortable, air-conditioned office is filled with tired workers, even after only a few hours of work. For contrast, take a look at this scene:

> A village in India. Early in the morning, with a plough on his shoulder and two bulls in front of him, the farmer walks to his plot of land. Where is this plot of land? Not one block away, but two-and-a-half miles away. There he ploughs from morning until noon and then eats what he has brought with him. He has been working in the hot sun. Ploughing is very strenuous work, and he feels exhausted, so he rests until 3:00. From 3:00 to 5:30 he ploughs again, and then, along with his bulls and with his plough on the shoulder, he walks two-and-a-half miles home.
>
> The amount of perspiration, the calories of physical energy

> that he spent in the field are incomparably greater than that of an office manager. When he reaches home, the farmer takes a bath, eats his dinner, and then joins his friends to sing in full-throated glee the whole evening long.

Where did the farmer get his energy? If he can have so much energy after toiling all day in the fields, why do we get fatigued so easily?

I am not trying to prove that people who complain of fatigue are not tired. They really are tired. But the farmer is not tired, because fatigue is not caused by physical exertion. Physical exertion cannot tire you, and if at all you feel any fatigue, one-half hour of rest will revive your physical body. The fatigue that we who live in the cities feel comes from mental exhaustion.

> The moment the store manager wakes up, he is worried about his position, about getting more clients, about getting better profits. Whatever he sees makes him worried. On the way to work, he sees someone with a Mercedes; he is worried that he cannot afford one. By the time he reaches the store, his energy has already ebbed out. In the store he feels worried because the owner has more money than he does. Thus, mentally he is already exhausted at the beginning of his workday, even though physically he has not done a bit of work.

The fatigue we feel in the modern world is not the fatigue of physical exertion, for with all the modern conveniences, physical exertion is unnecessary. Because of elevators, we need not climb stairs. Because of cars, we need not walk. All around us we have comforts to economize our precious energy, yet we complain that we have no energy at all!

The reason for the difference between the farmer and the store manager lies in the state of their minds. The simple farmer has a relatively clear and uncluttered mind. He leads a simple life and is happy with his simple comforts. When he ploughs with his bulls, he feels happy because they are his bulls. He ploughs for hours on end, and even if he should get physically tired, mentally he is enthusiastic, with his mind free of endless desires and dissatisfaction. In contrast, the store manager in our scenario is self-centered, and his mind is heavy with selfish desires. Anxiety about enjoyment of the results of his actions clutters his thinking. Desire and anxiety, two negative forces, sap his vitality. With such an agitated, tense mind, he cannot make progress either spiritually or materially.

Therefore, the secret of success lies in overcoming such a negative outlook. By making the mind more positive, we conserve our mental energy and thus have more energy to apply to action. In fact, unselfish actions help energize us toward even more dynamic activity. We can achieve this energizing effect by choosing an ideal in life high enough to boost us beyond our own selfish interests. If we work with constant dedication toward that high ideal, we will feel inspired in every activity. Besides having a more cheerful life, we will also have a better chance of being more successful at what we do.

An ideal is that which propels one to activity. In the case of a selfish person, his ideal is his own welfare. He does not make any efforts to help anyone beyond himself and his family. That same person can choose a higher ideal by creating a larger field of work. For instance, he can work not only for the welfare of his family, but that of his community also. When a person thus dedicates himself to a nobler cause, he becomes more efficient and successful. The one who represents the entire society is more dynamic in his efforts than the one who is self-centered.

The higher the goal, the greater will be our inspiration. As we serve the world, we discover new resources of energy welling up in us to pour out in tireless activity. Thus, it is necessary to have a clear and creative goal in life, so that we may look up to it and draw inspiration from it. As we discover such a goal and surrender ourselves to it, we unleash a new dynamo of energy within ourselves.

> A striking example of someone who found a great goal to inspire him was Mahatma Gandhi of India. Once he became energized by the goal to lead India to independence, he sacrificed his every comfort and risked his life for the sake of his nation, proving himself to be a person of great dynamism and strength, even though his outer life was very simple and humble.

When all the people of a given society dedicate themselves to an accepted ideal and gather the courage to live up to their convictions, then such a society is bound to grow into a dynamic and beautiful one. The development of beauty of personality at the individual level culminates in the birth of a beautiful, great society and a noble nation.

The ultimate ideal is to divert our attention from the body-mind-intellect to the Life Principle supporting them all, the unchanging factor of all life. The enlightened being is one who has chosen this highest Principle as his ideal and has dedicated all his activities to it. Such a person lives a life of total independence and is free from the influence of all changes, within and without.

For Your Study and Reflection

6. Action

STUDY QUESTIONS, Level 1

1. How would you classify yourself: as a laborer, a worker, or a person of achievement? Why?

2. Do you sometimes feel tired even though you've slept well the night before and have not had much physical exertion all day? Why do you think you feel tired at those times? What can you do to change that condition?

3. Think of a noble ideal you can set for yourself. What can you do in the next week or month to work for that ideal?

STUDY QUESTIONS, Level 2

1. If you cannot classify yourself as a person of achievement, what do you need to do to become one?

2. What happens in a mind filled with desires or filled with anxiety? What can you do to eliminate desiring or anxious thoughts from your mind?

3. Give examples of three people from current or past history who seem to have chosen high ideals to inspire their work. Cite evidence of how those ideals energized their actions.

FOR YOUR REFLECTION

- Verily, none can ever remain, even for a moment, without performing action, for everyone is made to act helplessly, indeed, by the qualities born of *prakṛti* (matter). (*Bhagavad Gītā* III:5)

- Perform your bounden duty, for action is superior to inaction. Even the maintenance of the body would not be possible for you by inaction. (*Bhagavad Gītā* III:8)

- Therefore, without attachment, always perform action that should be done, for by performing action without attachment man reaches the Supreme. (*Bhagavad Gītā* III:19)

FURTHER READING

- *The Holy Geeta* (*Bhagavad Gītā*). Commentary by Swami Chinmayananda. Bombay, India: Central Chinmaya Mission Trust, 1980. Chapter III, verses 3-26.

Values 7

Behind every achievement is the unseen hand of the human will. The cars in our garages, the television sets in our homes, the space shuttles probing the sky, and the vaccines developed against the most formidable of bacteria are all products crystallized out of the human will. Human will power and determination have conquered Nature and made her a slave for the welfare of humankind.

Much of what we see today as part of our abundant lives were only mere ideas yesterday in the minds of a few men and women. Those ideas would not have become a reality if those men and women had not had the will and determination to put their ideas into practice. The Hindu scriptures have given us examples of people of great will, such as Visvamitra, who could even create an entire new world out of his sheer power of willing. All people of great achievement have had the blessing of tremendous will power.

Truthfulness (*Satyam*)

The will to face the challenges we encounter is born out of our own courage of conviction. There are many dreamers, but few who realize their dreams. There are many chairside inventors, but few who bring their inventions into reality. Most of us, at the mere suggestion of a challenge to our ideas, fall ready victim to the challenge and are ready to compromise. The lives of all great people reveal to us that the basic necessity for the development of a strong will is the ability to live up to one's intellectual convictions and to act in harmony with them. When we live in the spirit of our intellectual convictions, we live in truthfulness (*satyam*).

> Margaret decides that she will dedicate all her free hours to help clean up the environment — to support the ecological health of her community. She begins to lobby the local organizations and to work with her colleagues in trying to get enough money raised and petitions signed to help put a major ecological issue on the next ballot. However, the local industries, with much to lose if the new legislation goes through, wage a major battle against the activists and succeed in publishing a series of inflammatory articles about the activist group, smearing their reputation in the eyes of the public. Margaret, convinced of the loftiness of her goal, does not allow this unfair attack to dishearten her and continues to fight vigorously for her ideal.

Only the intellect has the capacity to keep our values and ideals in place despite all external challenges. When we allow our ideals to be broken by our own weakness of mind, we compromise—and end up living a life of dishonesty (*asatyam*). When we thus compromise our convictions, we form a split in our personality, becoming cowardly in the face of further challenges in life.

The secret of success in life lies in keeping the head above the storms of the heart (the mind). A successful person never allows his discrimination and judgment to be disturbed by the rising tides of his emotions. When emotions and impulses start dictating our actions, we sink to the level of animals.

We must be ready to consider and reconsider an ideal for a thousand times if necessary, and in the light of all the evidence available, to accept or reject it. But once we accept an ideal as ours, we must discover in ourselves the heroism to live up to it at all times. This is called truthfulness, the source of the will and the courage to act upon our deepest convictions.

The most important trait in an eminently successful

person's life is integrity — an inflexible, undaunted, and firm integrity, or truthfulness at all levels of activity. Once an individual has developed in himself an indomitable integrity, he finds that he is the master of every challenge and every situation. And as others observe his efforts, they see in him a self-assurance that is both captivating and rewarding.

A person of integrity is accepted, believed, trusted, and befriended by all. To attract to oneself such genuine attitudes from others is to create and assure a vibrant environment for great undertakings and, with others' ready help, even for spectacular successes. Integrity is a personal asset for any person in any field.

The nobility inherent in integrity is rooted deep in the quality and beauty of our intentions. If the spring of our thoughts is pure and if we have the heroism to live unfailingly the great ideals we believe in, however impractical and utopian they may seem, even if immediate failures confront us, we will still have cultivated integrity, our great inner treasure. Thus, with each apparent failure, with each insurmountable obstacle, with each moment of social criticism, or even with merciless ridicule endured, we steel our nobility and reinforce our determination to live the honorable life, consistent with our ideal. Guided by such determination, our personality unfolds in glowing poise.

Such individuals alone are the true evolvers; all others are mere adapters. The adapters compromise at every turn, with every circumstance, ever struggling to readjust to the changing pattern of challenges. They may struggle on, helpless slaves to their habits, but they will never command the world to march to the appointed goal chosen by their own vision. Only a person of integrity has this power over life and its happenings. Naturally, then, integrity is the essential secret of an eminently successful life.

Self-Control (*Brahmacarya*)

We cannot achieve things in life by mere will power alone. After we develop the will to act according to our convictions, we have to find the energy required to produce the results we envision.

When we have no control over our sense organs, we have no control over the world. We become a slave to it. At the beck and call of the world, we let our energies run dry, dissipating all vitality from our personality. What remains is but a carcass of the physical body: a mere biological unit moving about, with its physiological activities intact but with no personality to assert, plan, or achieve. If a society is made up of such exhausted and empty human beings, no scientist can help improve it, no politician can save it, no economist can develop it.

> In the world of competitive sports, this fact is well known. Those who train athletes for the Olympic games prescribe a very strict regimen for their trainees: no smoking, no drinking, early bedtime, and a controlled and healthy diet. The trainers know that any excesses in the trainee's life will yield not only a weak body but also a weak mind, one not fit for the consummate concentration required for excellence in Olympic-level athletics.

The sages therefore advise us: Conserve your energies; don't allow them to be dissipated through the sense organs. This attitude of intelligent contact with the world outside is called *brahmacarya*.

Brahmacarya begins at the body level, in controlling the senses. For a beginner, it is impossible to observe *brahmacarya* at the mental level. The physical entity in us longs for contact with the world of objects to gain sense gratification:

- The eyes wish to see beautiful forms and colors.
- The tongue craves good food.
- The nose likes to smell pleasant fragrances.
- The skin invites soft sensations.
- The ears want to hear pleasing sounds.

When we live in continual seeking of gratification of our sensual demands, our passions ultimately consume us. We become slaves to our senses. To avoid such self-afflicted ills, the scriptures have prescribed *brahmacarya* as a discipline to be lived at the physical level.

Brahmacarya means living in self-control with respect to all of our sense enjoyments, but does not mean their total denial. The world of objects is meant for us to enjoy, and the scriptures do not deny us the freedom to enjoy it. But they do advise us to become *masters of our enjoyments* and not to allow them to enslave us. The sages beseech us,

> *"Enjoy the world, but let not the world enjoy you. Eat food, but let not the food eat you. Drink, but let not the drink drink you."*

As long as we can control our inner craving for enjoyment of sense objects — that is, as long as we neither long for enjoyment while not enjoying, nor forget ourselves as the masters of our senses while enjoying — we can afford to enjoy the world as much as we wish.

The interpretation of the word *brahmacarya* has been so badly distorted over the years that the real significance of this discipline has become lost. *Brahmacarya* is popularly misunderstood to mean complete abstinence from sexual life. This is absurd. What the sages advise us is to abstain from excessive indulgence in any sensual pleasure. In short, to talk too much or to listen to the radio all day means not to follow the principle of *brahmacarya*.

If we abruptly deny ourselves sensual pleasures to follow spiritual values blindly, the result is suppression.[1] When suppression continues for a period of time, we are led into a sense of bitterness, frustration, and cynicism. If, however, we follow the other extreme and indulge in sensual pleasures without setting any limits, the senses, being as

[1] Refer to the earlier discussion of suppression Chapter 4, "Balance."

strong and overpowering as they are, can pull us down into an abyss of animalism. Thereafter, any attempt to live a spiritual life is futile.

> Overindulgence is a frequent malady of modern life. Most people today are tempted to indulge themselves in sensual enjoyments recklessly and excessively. Television and radio ads coax us to do it, and billboards cajole us to indulge our senses to an ever-increasing degree. Those who end up submitting to temptation and indulge themselves to excess not only lose the little joy they had in their early contacts with the sense objects, but also deteriorate both at the physical and mental levels to such an extent that soon they become incapable of enjoying any sense objects at all. They live a jaded life.

Thus, the solution is to learn to regulate our physical indulgence, but not to deny it to the extent of causing suppression and frustration. Once we learn to regulate our conduct relative to sense enjoyments, we will win a greater capacity to enjoy our sense contacts. In addition, we'll gain the capacity to apply our faculties in other fields. No significant achievement in life, material or spiritual, is possible without this discipline.

We can control our senses by diverting our attention away from sense objects to the divine Principle that enlivens them all. *Brahmacarya* is the vow observed by a *brahmacārī*, and a *brahmacārī* is explained in Sanskrit thus: *brahmani carati iti brahmacārī*, "A *brahmacārī* is one who is constantly engaged in the contemplation of the Truth."

For a person who has understood that happiness lies in the mind, not in the objects of the world, *brahmacarya* is not a difficult discipline to practice. Once we learn, through *brahmacarya*, to conserve our inherent energy, we burst forth with a new dynamism and vitality. Such a dynamic, vitalized life is the life of *brahmacarya*. When a person combines such vitality with the courage to act on his convictions, success is inevitable.

Noninjury (*Ahiṁsā*)

At times we see a fine and dignified man of integrity, one serene in both storm and sunshine, beginning to decay, becoming weak, and even falling from his high pedestal of strength and glory. In the majority of cases, such falls are due to the fears that have stealthily laid their booby traps in the personality structure. If we carefully analyze such situations, we will find that all such cases have sprung forth from a *lack of charity*, a temporary incapacity to overlook some minor disappointment or the failure to disregard some words or actions of others. In a weak moment, when the person is off guard, any paltry happening can become a stupendous load on his mind. As he allows this dead weight of worry and agitation to drag him down, the man of integrity can no longer maintain his earlier poise.

To avoid such a calamity in ourselves, we must set up a free flow of forgiveness, with the help of which we can flush out all negativities. A person who is building himself up for the highest achievements must have the ability to forget the follies of others around him, the dishonesty of those who are working with him, and the vulgarities of the members of his team. All cannot have true inspiration, even when they are inspired. All may not have the capacity for real efficiency or the necessary constancy of purpose. Let us learn to forgive them; and if they continue to be bad, forget about them. As the poet says, "Good to forgive, best to forget."

The principle of noninjury (*ahiṁsā*) is: "In your mind, don't injure others." The masters of Vedanta commended this eternal value of life, beseeching us to live *ahiṁsā* at the mental level. This means: Never curse anyone, never wish harm to anybody. *Ahiṁsā* does not mean noninjury at the physical level. Sometimes we may have to injure another, even though the heart behind our actions is full of love.

> In *Hamlet*, Shakespeare beautifully expresses this idea: "I am cruel only to be kind." — *Hamlet* III:iv

> A common example from life is that of a surgeon operating on his patient. He may be physically hurting the patient and causing him pain, but, in fact, he means well. Such actions do not violate the principle of *ahiṁsā*.

At the mental level, let us at all times hold the positive thought of blessing everyone around us. Let our hearts flow out in love and kindness to all, wishing everyone welfare. While thus serving the world in the spirit of nonviolence, we may at times have to give a little pain to others, but only to bless them.

*

Satyam, *brahmacarya*, and *ahiṁsā* are the three cornerstones upon which the edifice of Hindu culture has been built. All scriptures growing out of that tradition are but an exposition of this set of triple values. Whenever these values are lived in a generation — whether at the individual, communal, or national level — we shall find a great blaze of joy and peace, love and serenity in the society. If the members of a community have no self-control at all, the community becomes wild. If they have no concept of noninjury toward other communities, no peace will prevail between the communities of the world. If a community has no conviction in its ideals, it cannot have a mutual and cohesive purpose.

Those generations that do decide to live according to these three values become healthy and strong to face not only the tragedies of their own times, but they also learn to enjoy a deep tranquillity in their entire historical era.

For Your Study and Reflection

7. Values

STUDY QUESTIONS, Level 1

1. Describe how lack of truthfulness (*asatyam*) can inhibit your pursuit of an ideal.

2. Give an example from your own life how self-control (*brahmacarya*) helped you attain a goal.

3. Give an example from your own life how not following the value of noninjury (*ahiṁsā*) affected your performance.

STUDY QUESTIONS, Level 2

1. Describe how the courage of one's convictions ties into the quality of truthfulness (*satyam*).

2. Explain, giving examples, how the values prescribed by Vedanta provide *practical* guidelines for living, as contrasted with abstract moral injunctions.

3. Why is it true that solely through detachment from the lower, without attachment to the Higher, one cannot easily reach a perfect state of *brahmacarya*? How does attachment to the Higher help in this effort?

FOR YOUR REFLECTION

- He whose mind is not shaken by adversity and who in prosperity does not hanker after pleasures, who is free from attachment, fear, and anger is called a sage of steady wisdom. (*Bhagavad Gītā* II:56)

- He who is everywhere without attachment, on meeting with anything good or bad, who neither rejoices nor hates, his wisdom is fixed. (*Bhagavad Gītā* II:57)

- When, like the tortoise, which withdraws its limbs on all sides, he withdraws his senses from the sense objects, his wisdom becomes steady. (*Bhagavad Gītā* II:58)

FURTHER READING

- *The Holy Geeta* (*Bhagavad Gītā*). Commentary by Swami Chinmayananda. Bombay, India: Central Chinmaya Mission Trust, 1980. Chapter XII, verses 13-19; Chapter XIII, verses 8-12.

Energy 8

Having developed the will, energy, and the right attitude for action by practicing *satyam*, *brahmacarya*, and *ahiṁsā*, a person can still be a failure in life — if she has not the efficiency to develop her talents and to funnel them out into the field of action.

What is this efficiency?

Efficiency: Dexterity in Action

Nature is ever prompt and efficient. We see efficiency at all levels of life: in the mineral, plant, and animal kingdoms. The happenings in the mineral world follow strict physical laws. Performance in the plant kingdom is ordered by the natural laws that regulate all plants. The bud on the apple tree matures in time, the flower blooms forth in time, the fruit ripens in time. The animals in their kingdom function impelled by the impulses of self-preservation, and the rhythm of their actions follows the law of the survival of the fittest.

The world of matter is utterly helpless relative to the physical laws, and blindly bound by them. In the plant kingdom there is a suffocating chain of environmental dictates. In the animal kingdom, some freedom enters in, but the animal world is still prompted largely by instincts and impulses. In the human being alone we detect the possibility of a mightier power with the help of which he can explode into victories over the very forces of nature and rise above the tyranny of his instincts and impulses. Herein lies the secret of efficiency, the secret of all great achievements by all evolved people of all eras.

Efficiency is the freedom to step up our own inherent abilities in the field of action. We express efficiency in the dynamism of our actions and in the cheerfulness of our work.

In the language of the rishis of India, the technique of attaining efficiency is called *yoga*: "Dexterity in action is yoga" — *yogaḥ karmasu kauśalam.*[1]

> A person like Albert Einstein is recognized as a genius in the West. In the yogic tradition, a genius is not born, but is the result of self-discipline, self-molding, and self-development. This approach is echoed in the words of another great mind from the West, Thomas Alva Edison, the inventor of the light bulb, who said, "Genius is one percent inspiration and ninety-nine percent perspiration."

A genius evolves through a process by which the source of dynamism latent in oneself is discovered, tapped, awakened, poured out, and utilized efficiently and to the best advantage. This involves three steps:

1. Generating dynamism
2. Conserving energy
3. Channeling energy into a chosen field of endeavor

We saw earlier[2] how we can generate dynamism (energy) in our work by choosing a higher ideal. However, sometimes we may feel momentarily inspired by an ideal, but once the source of that inspiration is gone, we are back again in the old lethargy. Where has that energy gone? The energy was with us, but it has been dissipated into various channels and is no longer available for the irrigation of our activity.

[1] *Bhagavad Gītā* II:50.
[2] In Chapter 6, "Action."

Right actions, done with the right attitude, enrich our vitality. Conversely, actions done with the wrong attitude dissipate our energy. All physical actions, mental feelings, and intellectual thoughts that spring from us — if sent out into the world with the wrong attitude, will recoil back upon us, causing agitation in the mind and creating regret and remorse. Actions that cause us remorse we call *sins* (*pāpa*). Actions that do not cause any regret but instead help to integrate our personality are called meritorious actions or *merits* (*puṇya*). Thus, *puṇya* and *pāpa* are *the reactions in the mind* of the actions we have done. Heaven and Hell are only two different mental states; they are not somewhere outside, but within ourselves.

> In a gush of anger I murder someone. The regret I feel afterwards, the mental torture I suffer at the deed I have done, in itself creates a Hell for me.

Action by itself is beyond good and bad. It is the attitude with which we do an action, the intention behind it, that matters.

Desire, hate, jealousy, passion — all such qualities drain our inner wealth and impoverish us. Affection, love, tenderness, peace, equanimity — these are all virtues (*puṇya*) that enrich our inner vitality. Therefore, we must be careful not to allow the energy we draw from our ideal to be misspent and wasted away in immoral and unethical pursuits.

It is a fact that the brute force of a cultivated will power is not always sufficient to stem the tide of our passionate tendencies. In one moment we may find ourselves drifting away irresistibly into our old habits of thinking and acting. And not too rarely, we detect our misconduct too late; we may find ourselves already having insulted our own clear understanding and firm determination by committing to a negative urge within us.

Therefore, we must learn to redeem our lower tendencies with emotions of a higher order. Let us open our head and heart to the enduring perfections and noble thoughts preached and lived by the wise seers of old. Such consistent exposure is sure to strengthen and purify our character. By repression of false tendencies we can never come out of their clutches; substitution of healthy ideas alone is the way to grow in our character. The best and easiest method of achieving this goal is to study the scriptures and reflect on their meaning.

In addition, we must stay alert to the energy leakages that may occur in our day-to-day life, even without our knowing.

Conserving Energy

Leakage of energy takes place through three dissipating channels. In our present mental condition, no sooner do we gain a fresh dose of energy than it dissipates through these three leakages. These energy drains are so serious that whatever may be the quantum of energy we gain, we manage to allow it to drain away immediately. We need to block these leakages and preserve the energy. If we succeed in doing that, our achievement is implicit and immediate. These three leakages are:

1. Regrets about a dead past
2. Anxieties about an imagined future
3. Feverish excitements in the present

For many of us, a major energy leakage is **regrets about the past**.

> Joe, an average student, decides that he must get the top grade on his next exam. He studies very hard for it, but as the examination time approaches, he thinks, "I have never received the top grade in the past. How can someone like myself ever expect to get it? I think I'll be satisfied with just a passing grade; I don't really need to get the top grade."

Thus, memories of a dead past manage to erode all of Joe's earlier confidence and energy.

Memories and regrets of the past form themselves into thoughts such as:

- "In the past I have always been late for every appointment; don't expect me to be different now."
- "Every time I've tried to change my habit of getting up late on Saturday morning, I've failed. I'll never be able to change that habit. I'm just not a morning person."

In this way, memories of the past come to disturb us, and our enthusiasm to face new challenges or meet new goals oozes away and our energy reserves run dry.

A second source of dissipation is **anxiety about the future**.

> Kamala, who has always been a top student, hopes to get top marks on her M.A. examination. The girl enters the examination hall rather pale, and the examiner thinks it is because of overstudy. When the question paper reaches the young student, she reads it and faints. The examiner rushes to her. Kamala says, "Please give me some water. I feel dizzy; I need to lie down." The girl moans in her mind, "Everything is lost. How can I answer fourteen questions when there is so little time — even though I know all the answers?" The girl, in her anxiety, had neglected to read the instructions, which said, "Answer any three questions"!

Because of Kamala's overanxiety to get the top grade, her efficiency was lost. Many students fail in their exams, not because they haven't studied, but because of such energy leakages that destroy their focus and sense of composure. In any situation, whether in the classroom or in the workplace or in the community, our success depends upon the mental equanimity with which we act.

Thus, dissipation of energy may take place either due to

lingering memories of the past or due to anxieties about the future. Even if these two are overcome, say the sages, we can still encounter a third cause of dissipation: **excitement in the present.** You may have noticed some people who sincerely work long hours, yet give a general impression of being extremely inefficient. No one wants to give such a person work.

> David works hard, no doubt, but he cannot come to any judgment. In the morning he looks at his desk: The files have already piled up, and he is worried about the amount of work. At that time, his secretary comes in with more files. By the time he starts working away at those files, he sees a "Rush!" label on another file. After reading it, he remembers the first file. Meanwhile, the secretary has brought him yet another file! He is worried and dejected. He doesn't know where to begin.

If David had had composure and self-confidence, he would have known that he should concentrate on one file at a time, come to a decision, and take action so that at least one file is disposed of. If he goes through his stack of memos and documents one by one, without becoming excited, he will find some efficiency in his work. But if he succumbs to the excitements of the present, they will dissipate his energy and destroy his efficiency.

To sustain the energy we've created, we must focus our entire energy on the activity we're engaged in — without letting our dynamism be eroded by any of the three main leakages. To focus our energy on what we are doing right now is the highest creative act in the world.

The Joy of an Artisan

When an individual has discovered new energy within himself, when he has learned the art of stopping the dissipation and is able to fix his entire energy on the piece of work at hand, a great joy starts welling up in his mind — the joy of an artisan. Such joy can be understood only by experiencing it.

For an artisan, drafting something new—whether the design for a toy or for an instrument of high precision—brings great joy and fulfillment.

To a large extent the mechanization of life in this technical age has robbed us of the joy that the artisan of the past experienced. In those days, when the artisan fashioned an article of furniture and the artist a piece of sculpture, they had the joyous satisfaction of *creating* something. Nowadays because of the division of labor and the introduction of increasing automation, the average worker has been robbed of her joy of creativity. Instead, an inert iron monster called a machine produces everything. Furniture is produced by machines; clothing is produced by machines. The worker thus does not have the joy of applying her creativity to her work. Instead, she programs and maintains machines. To that extent, the joy of creation has gone out of her life.

However, if we shift our perspective a little, we see that the joy of having done the right thing in the right way can still be ours. For example, even though typing is considered dreary work, if the typist executes his work neatly, without making mistakes, he earns his dividend of joy from having done his work well. We can discover joy in the precision and perfection of the work that we turn out, no matter what it may be. Whether others recognize it or not, we have the satisfaction that we did our work as well as we could, and a silent stream of joy fills our heart.

The artisan and artist who have been able to put their head and heart where their hands are working have discovered the joy of deep inner peace, a joy of religious ecstasy, because when the physical, mental, and intellectual personalities become integrated in an individual, he comes nearer to perfection. In that atmosphere of joy, the individual is capable of achieving his best.

Anyone who has a hobby can very easily understand this. A hobby means an activity of the hands and legs in which the head (intellect) and the heart (mind) concur. When the hands are doing something and the head and the heart are involved, the individual says that it is recreation, a hobby.

One man says that playing cricket from morning until evening is recreation. Another man calls playing football his recreation. A woman claims that playing tennis is her hobby. A young teenager insists that climbing sheer, vertical walls of rock, with backpack strapped to his back, is his greatest joy. If these same people were asked to exert that much energy to help a neighbor move some furniture or change a tire, they would resist: too energy-consuming! But in spite of the amount of energy and perspiration they may have spent on a tennis court, a football or cricket field, or a mountainside, they come away saying that they feel revived and full of energy.

> On summer vacations, South Indian teenagers often go to North India for a holiday. They sightsee the whole day and walk along deserted roads in midday heat. The local people are afraid of sunstroke, and when they look out of their windows to see these teenagers walking without any protection, they wonder, "How is it that they are walking in the sun?" They close their windows and rest in the assumption that South India is probably hotter and therefore these youngsters are walking comfortably in the cooler sun of North India.
>
> But the teenagers don't even notice that it is hot. They are living in a realm of their own. They have come to the North to sightsee, and however uncomfortable the heat may be, it is fun for them because their purpose is to enjoy the holiday. Thus, walking in the hottest sun, sleeping in railway stations, catching any train, and suffering in many ways all comprise an enjoyable adventure, for their heads and hearts are present where their physical bodies are engaged in action.
>
> After the teenagers have returned home, if the old grandfather of one of them were to ask him to get something from the corner store, the boy will complain that the sun is too hot! He forgets that when the thermometer was at 114° F he was walking five miles on the tarred road of Agra in North India, enjoying himself all the way. Here the thermometer is a mere 80° F, yet he feels too hot to run an errand for his grandfather.

You and I often feel disappointed in life, not because

there is no meaningful work in the world but because we are not discovering work in which the functions of the physical body are in harmony with the head and the heart. The person who can bring all these three aspects of the personality together in one field of activity works in an inspired manner. Inspired work not only brings forth higher productivity and efficiency, but also provides a great dividend of joy for the worker. To work in this way is the art of living, described in detail in the Vedas, and especially in the immortal poem called the *Bhagavad Gītā*.

Channeling Energy

In summary, according to the great masters, we should first discover a goal from which to draw our inspiration. Once we have found that goal or ideal, whether it is political, economic, or spiritual, if it is an ideal that we have chosen according to the nature of our heart — not one that somebody imposed on us — then a new enthusiasm floods our mind. And once we have enthusiasm, then sincerity, ardor, and consistency of purpose automatically follow. Next, we need to channel our energy to achieve our goal without dissipating our vitality through unintelligent regrets of the past, futile imaginations about the future, or frenzied excitements in the present.[3] If we work on in the world with our head, heart, and hands fully integrated, the very work gains a stamp of efficiency and beauty — and our reward is an indescribable feeling of fulfillment and joy.

[3] In Chapter 9, "Mind," and Chapter 11, "Vāsanās," we will study in greater detail ways to control the mind and conserve our energy.

For Your Study and Reflection

8. Energy

STUDY QUESTIONS, Level 1

1. Take five minutes to watch your mind. As you witness the flow of thoughts, make a mental note about the kind of thoughts you encounter: Are they about the past, the future, or the present?

2. Recall the definition of a "hobby" relative to the functioning of the physical body and the mental equipment. Why do people find hobbies enjoyable?

3. When do you feel most happy while working on something? Why?

STUDY QUESTIONS, LEVEL 2

1. How do you think we can rid ourselves of the habit of dwelling much of the time on the past or worrying about the future?

2. Describe how an activity can be transformed into inspired work.

3. Recall in your mind a person you know or have heard about who has a joyful attitude toward work. Describe

his attitude and approach toward work and explain how it seems to affect his efficiency and effectivenesss.

FOR YOUR REFLECTION

- There is no educated man who has not the competence to act and to achieve. Everyone is competent in his own limited field, yet, while working therein, many prove indeed very inefficient. Competence arises from technical know-how — from the general theoretical information and facts gathered and remembered through the patient and analytical observation of one's own an others' experiences in the field. Yet with all this knowledge, the intelligent individual can still prove to be inefficient in his chosen field of action.

  Efficiency is the capacity in an individual to funnel his available *competence* into the field of action. An intelligent preparedness is called *competence,* and when this ultimately reaches the field of our action, it expresses as our *efficiency*. The vital artery that carries out competence into the actual field of work is our mind. Therefore, mental discipline is the secret of all efficiency, the end product of all poised competence. In the spiritual world this is equally true: If the seeker is not efficient, he is incapable of ever reaching his final goal.

  Systematically, therefore, we must train and discipline the mind for right thinking and for correct and diligent activity. Right thinking is a habit that can be cultivated. Substitution of positive thoughts for negative ones and flooding the mind with creative ideas are methods by which we can flush out the floor of the mind, littered as it is now with the filth of incomplete thoughts and decaying ideas. Having recognized a thought to be negative or wrong, do not waste time in upholstering it to look neat and attractive, but reject it immediately and totally. The power of right thinking expels all false thoughts and induces healthy concepts to rise. (Swami Chinmayananda, *We Must,* pages 32-33)

FURTHER READING

- Swami Chinmayananda, *We Must*. Napa, California: Chinmaya Publications West, 1976. Chapter 9.

Mind 9

Our age-old habit is to turn our minds outward at all times. We have not yet learned to turn them inward. We have not yet learned to use our discriminating intellects to discover the nature of our thoughts and to find out what makes up the world of our daily experiences.

Experiencing the World

Our three kinds of equipment are the body, the mind, and the intellect, and with them we meet all experiences in life. Through these three instruments life is constantly pulsating in and through us. When life is working through the physical body, we perceive the world of objects. When life functions through the mind, we experience the world of feelings; and when life expresses itself through the intellect, we comprehend the world of ideas or thoughts.

BODY	MIND	INTELLECT
|	|	|
World of Objects	World of Emotions	World of Thoughts

Each person has a distinctive set of these three instruments of the body, mind, and intellect. Hence, each person is a unique personality. Our total world of experiences is made up of our world of objects, our world of feelings, and our world of thoughts. All these put together constitute our total field of experience.

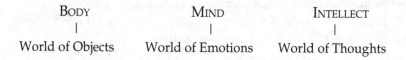

The art of living is the art of tuning our three instruments properly so that through them we may have a proper experience of the world. For the objective scientists, knowledge of the outer world is the goal. The subjective scientists, on the other hand, declare that to live purposefully we must unfold the knowledge of our inner selves. Through that knowledge alone can we learn to establish the right relationship to the world around us.

Let us consider for a moment what the politician, the economist, and the scientist achieve in this world:

- Politicians order our relationship to the people around us.
- Economists regulate our relationship to the wealth in the country.
- Scientists command our relationship to the physical phenomena.

Thus, in all aspects of life, we are being educated in how to relate ourselves to the world so that we may learn to live harmoniously in it. Two factors exist in this situation: the world and ourselves. The world around us is not fully under our control, but if we can each reorganize our inner life, we may learn to gain a glorious and healthy harmony in every aspect of our existence.

Four Personalities

In their analysis of the human personality and how it relates to experience, the ancient masters saw that even though each person is physically one being, various subtle aspects of his reaction to the objects of the world make him a composite structure of four different personalities:

- The physical (the most gross layer of the four)
- The mental
- The intellectual
- The spiritual (the most subtle layer of the four)

When an individual, the subject, comes in contact with an object of experience, he does so, not as an integrated whole, but as a collection of four "mouths" ready to enjoy that object. Four different layers of personality within himself, each with its own distinctive values and demands, rise up at the challenge of each situation in the outer world.

> Your neighbor offers you a piece of sumptuous chocolate cake covered with a thick layer of whipped cream. The physical person in you at once jumps up to experience it: The eyes register the shape, the nose takes in the fragrance, and at the mere sight of the cake, the tongue starts watering. The mental personality also rushes forth to experience the delectable offering. The intellectual faculty as well rises up to evaluate the situation, but it remembers the warning of your doctor that too much sugar is not good for you. The spiritual personality may also have its say: It may declare that allowing yourself to be tempted by sense objects may lure you away from the true locus of happiness, which does not reside in any object outside yourself.

Thus, at every moment, in each experience, four different faculties are at play. Often, that which brings satisfaction to one of the four personalities conveys but varying degrees of dissatisfaction to all the other three. However, the ancient sages also discovered that the human being is always ready to sacrifice the demands of the grosser personality to those of the subtler one.

> If an ulcer on one of your limbs causes you unbearable pain, you will accept the doctor's advice to sacrifice the limb to amputation, if need be, in order to divest your mind of the pain you're experiencing. For the sake of an intellectual conviction — say, a social or political cause — you may even find yourself ready to sacrifice the emotional security of the family and the physical comforts of a home. The martyrs of history have often made such sacrifices for the sake of an intellectual or spiritual objective.

Thus, psychological satisfaction is richer than physical gratification. And the subtler the personality level, the greater the satisfaction. Thus, as we identify with the subtler in us — with the intellectual personality rather than the body or the mind; or with the spiritual part of ourselves, rather than with the intellect or the mind — we not only integrate the lower layers into the more subtle ones, but also learn to experience the world in a more subtly joyous way.

Right Thinking

We recognize or experience the world never as such, but only as interpreted by our instrument of experience, the mind.

> To the scientist, the world is an expression of physical forces, a world to be categorized, dissected, and documented. When the botanist walks down the garden path and gazes at the fragrant blossom of a flower, he notes the petals, the stamen, the stigma, the pistil. When a lover walks down that same garden path and sees that same flower, his mind fills with thoughts of his beloved as he sees her beauty reflected in the graceful curvature of the delicate petals of the blossom.

The objects remaining the same, from person to person the experiences are different, since each experiencer is not merely the physical body, but also the mind and the intellect. And the very same objects that ordinarily give us joy, under circumstances of fear and sorrow, yield us pain instead. Thus we find that the world has the capacity to make us smile in joy or weep in sorrow — merely be reaching us through the mind. As the mind, so the world.

When we reach this much understanding of the process of perception and experience, it becomes clear that our lives will be filled with joy if our minds are tuned in such a way as to give us always an experience of happiness and peace. The attempt of religion is to bring this joyful balance to our minds.

Knowing that our minds literally determine the nature of our lives, many questions may plague us:

- How do I prepare for my actions in the world?
- How can I get my mind to follow my bidding?
- How can I improve the daily contacts in my life?

All of us would like to improve ourselves. We know that at times we lose our temper, even with dear ones, such as brothers and sisters, parents, or spouses. Perhaps no one at home takes us seriously, and we begin to despair:

> "No one understands me. I'm unhappy. A hundred things are going wrong. My life is a total mess. I feel so miserable. What's wrong with me?"

When we feel such depth of miserable emotion, we are experiencing negative qualities of the mind. When we start expressing negative emotions, others feel repelled. If we can learn to bring into expression the fragrance of the positive qualities of the mind, then other people will rush toward us, charmed by our beauty and grace.

Positive attracts positive: This has been found true all over the world, whether in South Africa or New York or Bombay. In whatever society, of whatever caste, creed, or color, people are magnetically pulled by certain qualities. The qualities that attract others are called *positive qualities*. When we deal with others, if we open up the sweetness of our personality, more people circle around us, love us, and are ready to support our creative programs.

Such positive qualities lie dormant in all of us, but they are often not invoked. It is not sufficient that we merely know of these things. Every one of us knows about love, mercy, cheer, kindness, joy, and the courage of conviction. We know that all of these are noble virtues; we recognize them as the qualities we admire in others, but when we act, we compromise our ideals.

Why?

We have wonderful ideas, but the instrument called the mind is not available to us for the execution of those ideas. Therefore, the sages declared: Unless we can learn to master the mind, unless we gain control over the instrument of expression, we cannot translate our ideas into appropriate action. Failure in the world is never due to lack of ideas. Most of us are bestowed with wonderful ideas, but when we try to put them to work, to express them in the society, somehow or other they go wrong and we end up not succeeding.

The mind is the instrument that translates into action the ideas and convictions of the intellect. In our home we learned from our parents and from books; in school, we learned from teachers and more books. From these we got the bulk of our intellectual ideas. We understood them and analyzed them in our head. However, whatever mass of knowledge we may have acquired, we can still be utter failures in life unless we can learn to make manifest that knowledge in our lives. In order to send the knowledge out into the world, we have to direct it through our mind. Therefore, mental control — mental development — is of utmost importance. The student who develops a certain amount of mind control is the one who will meet with the greatest success in life. This idea, developed throughout the ages by the great rishis of Vedanta, is called *yoga*. Disciplining the mind is yoga—not that which is popularly called yoga, that is, sitting with folded legs, nose held between two fingers.

How is the mind to be disciplined? In order to discipline the mind, we must first know what the mind is.

The Nature of the Mind

If the mind is happy, we are happy. If the mind is unhappy, we are unhappy. Our entire life is dependent on the mind, but very few of us know it. That fact is not taught in college. When we ask the question, "What is the mind?" an intelligent person will probably answer, "Mind is thought." Yes, whenever there are thoughts, we can say that the mind exists. Whenever there are no thoughts, we can say there is no mind. In deep sleep no thoughts exist, and therefore there is no mind.

Thus, thoughts and the mind are very much interrelated. If the thoughts are calm, the mind is calm. If the thoughts are agitated, the mind is agitated. If the thoughts are hopeful, the mind is hopeful. The mind is exactly as the thoughts in it.

However, thought alone is not the mind. The sages of India concluded that the thoughts and the mind have a relationship similar to that of water and the river:

> Water by itself is not a river. A pool of water is not a river. However, when waters flow in a continuous stream, a river is born. Thus, a river is water flowing. Similarly, thought by itself is not the mind, but when thoughts flow, the mind exists.
>
> When the waters of the river are muddy, the river is called muddy. When the waters are clean, the river is clean. When the waters are fast, the river is fast. As the waters, so the river.
>
> Similarly with the mind: as the thoughts, so the mind. If the thoughts are good, the mind is good. If the thoughts are bad, the mind is called bad. A person may have a beautiful body, a big car, and a million dollars, but if his mind is unhappy, he is unhappy. If the mind is good, the whole world is attracted to the owner of that mind.

We can understand the mind further by understanding its relationship to the intellect. We can think of the mental function as the expression of thoughts in two different ways:

Thoughts as emotions	= the mind (*manas*)
Thoughts as ideas or decisions	= the intellect (*buddhi*)

We can understand the differences between these two aspects of the mental function by again using the analogy of the river:

Mind	*Intellect*
A flow of thoughts, like the flow of water in a river	That which directs the thoughts, just like the banks of a river direct the water in it

Training the Mind

We must therefore train the mind for right thinking, a habit that can be cultivated, just like the habit of locking the door of the house as you leave it. Some approaches to training the mind are:

- Negating negative thoughts

  When a negative thought comes into the mind, reject it immediately and totally.

- Substituting positive thoughts for negative thoughts

  In place of the negative thought rejected, immediately substitute a positive thought.

- Flooding the mind with creative ideas

  To keep negative thoughts from invading your mind, fill the mind with positive ideas of creative vigor.

By such methods, we can flush out the floor of the mind, littered as it is now with the filth of incomplete thoughts and decaying ideas. We can sweep the mind clean and reenergize it with vibrant, life-bestowing thoughts.

In later chapters, we shall look in more detail at various practical means for controlling the mind. At this point, let's consider how best to develop the knack for looking within, for changing the mind's habit of always turning outward.

Looking Within

Just as an infant needs help in learning to recognize things and then later must learn to stand on its own tiny feet and walk across the length of the room, so too the newborn spiritual aspirant must first learn to recognize the world within and then learn to walk among the sense objects of the world. And just as a well-fed baby lies cheerfully kicking its limbs in the air while its eyes are fixed upon the light of the lamp above his head, so too, the aspirant must learn to go about the business of daily life while uninterruptedly watching the mind within.

> Each thought, word, and deed should emerge from you bearing the seal of your own recognition. Post a portion of your attention as a sentry on the watchtower of your intellect. Let it be a silent observer of the machinations of the mind: the motives, intentions, and purposes that lie behind your every thought, word, and deed.

With the intellect thus alerted to stand witness to your mind's proceedings, no activity issues forth from you unconsciously. You are ever awake to the goings-on in your mind. In the evening, make a habit of the following practice:

> At the close of each day, order a parade of your day's activities within your mind: all thoughts, words, actions, and emotions that transpired in the course of the day. Stand apart from them all and impartially review your day's events as a silent witness. Don't stop at any event to think about it; merely witness the event and move on.

This is called **introspection.** Practice it daily. Start today. The tomorrow you are waiting for may never come.

In the beginning, the attempts at self-analysis may prove disheartening. Your first few days' report of your analysis may read as the narration of the ideal life of a saint. Never mind; continue the daily practice. Soon you'll discover weaknesses, faults, and animalisms in each day's transaction. This is called **detection.**

Within a week's time you'll discover that yours is not,

after all, a saint's life. Such a revelation comes to even the best of aspirants. Do not let such dark reports discourage you. The darker the report, the greater should be your effort in readjusting your values and redirecting your thought currents.

Inner reformation always comes as a result of revelation. The moment you have detected your weaknesses and are really ashamed of them, that very moment those wrong traits die. This is called **negation.**

Yet, this is only half the battle won. In the wake of each victory comes the task of constructive peace. As soon as you apprehend a weakness and defeat it, substitute its opposite virtue in your personality. As you continue this process in your day's dealings, you will find the new quality growing and becoming part of your natural character. This is called **substitution.**

Self-analysis is the open door of welcome for all aspirants who may hesitate in awe at the courtyard of the temple — the Life Divine. If you start your practice of personality rehabilitation with daily introspection, you ensure yourself against all future melancholy feelings of futility and failure. Remember:

- Introspect daily
- Detect diligently
- Negate ruthlessly
- Substitute wisely

Grow steadily — and become happy, free, and successful in every aspect of your life.

Inner and Outer

Our physical pose and poise can generate a corresponding attitude in the mind.

> Look in a mirror while keeping your face contorted into a sorrowful expression. Maintain that expression for two or

three minutes and then watch your mind. Is it not feeling despondent, miserable, and dejected?

Now look in the mirror again and smile. After a minute of joyful smiling, watch and discover that the mind has caught the cheer in the face and is rippling away in joy.

The physical movements in ritualism were conceived on the basis of this interaction of the outer and the inner. The movements we follow in religious ritual help to bring into expression the correct attitude (*bhāvanā*) of the mind, the goal of all spiritual practices:

> The feeling of freshness after the bath, the reserved space for prayer, the burning of fragrant incense, the sandalwood paste on the forehead, the sparkling lamps, the decorated altar, the hymns sung, the mantra chanted — all are meant to create the correct external atmosphere to establish the required mental attitude.

Just as our mental moods determine our actions, our physical attitude can, in turn, induce a mental mood in us. Of the two, strengthening the right physical habits is easier; and once the physical habits are set, training the mind becomes more simple and sure.

> Watch your posture both standing and sitting, deliberately straightening the backbone whenever you find yourself slouching. Remember that when your body is erect, your organs perform their physiological functions more efficiently. Carry your head erect, shoulders well pushed back, chest always high. Breathe consciously, taking deep, health-bestowing breaths.

Conversely, glowing, optimistic thoughts, heroic ideals, and divine ideas have a powerful and uplifting effect on the body. Hopeful plans lend a spring to our stride and an attractive buoyancy to our dash into the daily fields of work.

Constant and alert **vigilance** over our thoughts and

actions is the price we have to pay for the greater prize of a happy, accomplished life. Patient self-application, in full enthusiasm and in a joyous mood of healthy optimism, is the plan of action of all great achievers in this world.

For Your Study and Reflection

9. Mind

STUDY QUESTIONS, Level 1

1. Describe one instance when a happy state of mind rendered the world you saw around you especially beautiful. Describe another instance when an upset mind colored everything you saw as though filled with misery. What does this tell you about the nature of the world?

2. Recall an event in which you sacrificed a lower level of your personality (for instance, the physical layer) to a higher level. Describe the effects.

3. Describe the three steps of the introspection process.

STUDY QUESTIONS, Level 2

1. Explain, with examples, the meaning of "As the mind, so the world."

2. Why is it not enough just to negate negative thoughts? Why is substitution of positive thoughts necessary?

3. Describe the role of vigilance in bringing your mind under control.

FOR YOUR REFLECTION

- If the mind ever so slightly strays from the ideal and becomes outgoing, then it goes down and down, just like a ball bounces down from one step to another after being inadvertently dropped on a flight of stairs. (Shankaracharya, *Vivekacūḍāmaṇi* 325)

- Thus, always keeping the mind balanced, the yogi, with his mind controlled, attains to the Peace abiding in Me [the Lord], which culminates in total liberation. (*Bhagavad Gītā* VI:15)

- When the perfectly controlled mind rests in the Self, free from longing for all objects of desire, then it is said: "He is united." (*Bhagavad Gītā* VI:18)

FURTHER READING

- Swami Chinmayananda, *Meditation and Life*. Piercy, California: Chinmaya Publications West, 1992. Chapter 7, "How to Begin."

Karma 10

Once we understand how our unmanifest urges, our *vāsanās*, drive our actions, we may hastily conclude that we are helpless victims of our *vāsanās*, that we have no choice in our actions but are destined to act according to the push of our innate urges.

In animals this inevitability is true. For instance, a carnivorous animal has the tendency to strike and kill, and all its actions follow that innate pattern. It has little discretion to live apart from its ferocious and destructive nature. However, the human being, the sovereign of creation, has the unique capacity to stand apart from his surging desires and exercise **self-effort** (*puruṣārtha*), which helps him choose actions regardless of his *vāsanās*. By consistent self-effort, the human being can successfully eradicate his *vāsanās* and transform his life.

The Law of Karma

Certainly, even as we apply our self-effort, our *vāsanās* — the effects of our past — have a pull on us in the present. After all, the present is the product (or effect) of our entire past. We are what we are because of our past actions.

> If my experiences up to the present moment have been pure and noble, today I am a person of chastity and dignity. But if my experiences have been vicious and immoral, I take on those qualities in my present life.

In short, we are the product (or effect) of our own past actions, or karma. This is the principle of **destiny** (*prārabdha*), one aspect of the **Law of Karma**.

Each human being represents the various effects arising from different causes. The causes being different, the effects are different. Thus, every action of the past has its own reaction, and each of us must have a treasury of such past reactions.

> Suppose I have a plot of land divided into orchards. In one, I plant coconut seedlings; in the second, apples; and in the third, mangoes. In order to germinate, grow, and yield fruit, each seed must take its own time.
>
> Similarly, each action takes its own allotted time to fructify — to yield a reaction, an effect. Every action has its own reaction. Certain actions give their reactions immediately, while others give their reactions only after an interval.

To live out the reactions of our past actions, we need to experience certain joys and sorrows, and in order to bring forth these required experiences we must have a definite field for our experiences.

We have come into this world to enjoy and suffer for certain of our past actions (karmas) through the circumstances ordered by our *prārabdha*. Still, we have the freedom to discriminate and to act nobly and in a wholesome way in any situation that arises:

- Don't we have a certain amount of freedom of choice in deciding whether we go to a movie or a store or to a church or a temple?
- Can't we make a decision between reaching for the rich sweet or the plate of fresh fruit slices?
- Don't we have a choice to decide whether to bombard a friend with an angry outburst or to say a kind word to her instead?

Nature has given us a certain amount of freedom:

> We cannot bend a piece of thick metal, but if we beat and shape the metal to form a chain, it becomes pliable. Again, when a cow is tied to a rope in the center of a pasture, it is not free to graze across the entire field but can move freely within the circle drawn by the rope. Similarly, although we have taken a certain form to live out a given *prārabdha*, we can apply our pure motives and intelligent discrimination to harness the freedom allowed us from moment to moment.

Self-Effort

As we have already seen,[1] two distinct paths are open to us, the path of the good and the path of the pleasant. We find ourselves at every moment standing at the junction of these two paths. Often we are at a loss to decide which path to pursue. By adopting the path of the pleasant, we can get immediate but short-lived rewards, whereas by adopting the path of the good, we can gain the long-term goal — permanent, unadulterated happiness. Thus, at each moment, we can exercise our self-effort to choose the right path for ourselves.

> Imagine that the mind is made up of soft matter. As each thought passes through it, an impression, like a scratch, is left on it. When similar thoughts are repeated, the small scratch deepens into a canal. Every subsequent thought has a tendency to flow through that ready-made thought canal. Thus, if the impression, or canal, was produced by good thoughts, then a good character is maintained and strengthened by the subsequent thoughts flowing irresistibly in that direction.

If you have a tendency to get angry and want to overcome that tendency, the first step is to feel repentant about it. Just feeling repentant will dissipate your anger to some

[1] In Chapter 4, "Balance."

extent. However, if you merely suppress the anger, it will burst forth at a later date. But if you are intelligent, you divert that energy in some other profitable direction. You should not succumb by meekly saying, "It is my *prārabdha* to get angry."

Carve out a new canal in your mind with repeated good thoughts. Repeat to yourself, "I love all," "I am very tolerant," and so on. Repeat these thoughts full of suggestion over and over again, and in a short time you will observe that you have no anger at all in your mental make-up.

Cause and Effect

To understand the cause-effect relationship better, let us look at the rules that such a relationship must follow:

1. There can be no effect without a cause.
2. The effect is none other than the cause itself in another form.
3. When the cause is removed from the effect, nothing of the effect can remain.
4. Therefore, the cause is concurrent with and inherent in the effect.

The play of cause and effect can only take place in the medium of time. First must be the cause, followed by the effect. The past is the cause and the present is the effect; and the present itself becomes the cause with reference to the future. Since we exist in the present, we are not only the effect of our past, but we are also the cause for our future.

By looking back at our past, we are helpless victims of our past actions. From this limited perspective we are bound by our dead past. However, the Law of Karma does not stop there. It says that if we look ahead (instead of behind us at our past), we become the architects of our own future. When we choose our present actions by applying self-effort, we create a future of our choice. All through our life, we have been exercising this capacity of self-effort to some degree; all past self-efforts combined have determined our present destiny. In other words, the sum total of all self-efforts (*puruṣārtha*) is equal to our present destiny (*prārabdha*). Thus we can say:

- *What* we meet in life is destiny.
- *How* we meet what we meet is self-effort.

If we have chosen the path of the pleasant in the past, we have to suffer the consequences of that in the present; but our self-effort today can be applied to choosing the path of the good, which combines with the past and creates a future better than our present. The future, therefore, is the continuity of the past modified in the present.

> The rate of flow of water in a river is 2 miles an hour. A log of wood floating on the water will also move at the same speed as the water in the river. If the log is fitted with a motor with an independent speed of 10 miles an hour, its speed will, in effect, be conditioned by the flow of the river. Its independent speed is no doubt 10 miles an hour, but when it is directed downstream, it registers 12 miles an hour, and when it is diverted upstream, the speed is reduced to 8 miles an hour.

The animal and plant kingdoms, like pieces of logs, merely float down the river of life without any freedom to change the course of their travel. The human being, however — the log with a motor — has his discriminating intellect with which to choose to apply his self-effort to modify the course set by the river. Just as the motorized log has an independent speed, so also our self-effort is independent of destiny. As we apply that self-effort against the background of our destiny, the effect produced by self-effort is modified by the past, but it is no longer determined solely by the past.

Thus, if we look at life from the perspective of destiny only, we are victims of our past; however, the Law of Karma infuses the spirit of creation into our lives by focusing our attention on the future.

Creating the Future

The human intellect cannot rest without seeking the cause of things, but we generally do not take full advantage of this causation-hunting urge in us. If we search for the causes of our present life, we shall discover certain facts that reveal to us the inner meaning of the Law of Karma.

- From the seed the tree grows:

  The seed is the cause, and the tree is the effect.

- From cotton cloth is made:

  Cotton is the cause, and cloth is the effect.

In all conceivable examples, the cause comes first in reference to time, like the father of a child; and the effect comes second, like the child born. The father was in existence before the child was born. Cause is that which was, and the effect is that which is. The past causes the present; the present will, therefore, cause the future.

In short, it is said that the future is not a mystery — an unknown miracle that we must wait to see unfold. Instead:

The past modified in the present is the future.

The things to come are not ordered by a mere continuity of the past. This freedom to modify the past and thereby to create a future for better or for worse is called self-effort.

To consider that the present is but a product of the past is undignified. To recognize that the future is only a product of the present actions is unintelligent. There is no slavery, nor is there complete freedom. There is, however, a limited freedom. If we use that freedom intelligently, we can redeem ourselves from all entanglements.

Thus, the Law of Karma, when properly understood, is a great, vital force. It makes us the architects of our own future.

We are not helpless pawns in the hands of a mighty tyrant. If we are weak or sorrowful, it is solely because of our own willful actions. In our ignorance, we may have pursued certain negative values of life in the past, and their fruits have reared up now to give us the pattern of circumstances we are living in today.

Take heart. By living rightly today the divine values of love, kindness, tolerance, and mercy, you will ensure a more noble pattern for your future. By honest introspection, you can detect your wrong tendencies and eliminate them through constant, deliberate effort. Develop positive thinking and thus become the creator of your own future life.

The Law of Karma applies not only to an individual, but also to communities and nations. And again, it does not have to apply to the present age only; it can embrace past and future ages as well. In this way, the Law of Karma enables us to view life in its entirety, providing a new meaning, purpose, and rhythm to our existence. To try to understand life without applying the Law of Karma is like seeing a life-size painting with eyes fixed a few inches from the canvas. From such a perspective, we see only a narrow, constricted view of life; the vision of the totality is lost to us.

We think that life means only the period spent by us from our birth to our death and that what we experience during this interval is the sum total of life. But when we extend the Law of Karma to its logical end, we have to conclude that it would be illogical to confine this law to the present life only. The effects we experience in our present life must have had their causes in a past life or lives, and the causes we create in the present life will surely grow into effects to be lived not only in the future years of this life, but also in future lives. For that reason, the Indian rishis formulated the idea of rebirth, concluding that all of us pass through countless births, lives, and deaths. The repeated passing of an individual soul through cycles of reincarnation constitutes *saṁsāra*, the endless cycle of births and deaths we all experience until we realize our identity with the supreme Reality.

The example of a picture painted on a vast canvas provides a telling analogy to viewing our life from the perspective of its entirety:

> The canvas is huge, with many people pictured on it against the background of a city perched on a hill. If we keep our eyes glued close to the canvas, we see coarse patches of paint and unintelligible shapes. In order to decipher the shapes and then to see the entire picture painted on the canvas, we have to step back some distance. Only then can we see the entire view: the rhythm of the colors, the beauty of the shapes, the majesty of the composition.

Similarly, when we view life from a close perspective, we feel that it is illogical and unrhythmic. But when we stand back from the current situation in detachment and try to view the whole of life in its entirety, we begin to perceive a vast harmony and perfection.

Some of us blame the Creator for the sorrow or sin in our lives and say that the sorrows have been fated upon us. The masters of Vedanta teach differently. It is important that we understand that there is a rhythm in the universe, that the planets move regularly, that the stars ride their appointed paths, and that the natural laws never deviate from Nature. Everywhere we can discover the law of rhythm, and everything conforms to that law — including our lives.

Humans that we are, let us never look back for a moment but dynamically march forward, creating a glorious future of magnificent achievements by exercising the unique capacity in our minds — self-effort.

For Your Study and Reflection

10. Karma

STUDY QUESTIONS, Level 1

1. Describe the difference between the Law of Karma and the Law of Destiny.

2. Describe the rules that govern cause and effect.

3. Recall an incident from your own life when, through self-effort, you changed an established pattern. How did that self-effort change your future course of action?

STUDY QUESTIONS, Level 2

1. In view of the Law of Destiny and the Law of Karma, would you say there is free will? Why or why not?

2. How does the Law of Karma "infuse the spirit of creation into our lives"?

3. Analyze an event or an epoch in the history of a given country that illustrates the workings of the Law of Karma.

FOR YOUR REFLECTION

- "Grace of the self, grace of God, grace of the guru, and grace of the scriptures — those who have gained these four realize the Truth and rejoice beyond the shadow of fear." This is a common saying of the ancient sages. Of these four, grace of the self means self-effort. God helps those who help themselves. By the grace of God an aspirant comes into contact with a guru who is established in God-consciousness. Through the grace of the guru, he learns the values of the spiritual life. Then, with his own free will, he puts what he has learned into practice. Thus he reaches the state of God-realization. At the root of all gain is self-effort. Devote your days and nights to spiritual exercises. You will be, in the end, crowned with success. (Swami Tapovanam, *Guidance from the Guru*)

- The present alone is the time when we can work and achieve, gain and gather, give and serve. In the past we can *now* do nothing; in the future, again, we can *now* accomplish nothing. In the dead moments of the past and in the unborn moments of the future, we can never act. These living, dynamic, present moments are the only fields to be hammered at, wherein lie all the glories of life, all the gains in existence.

  From the future, time floods over us, who are now standing in the present, and gushes out to swirl with the continuous echoes of the past. Time never stops; it is ever fleeting. The *now* alone is the auspicious occasion for initiating our new plans. Delays are always dangerous, useless, barren. Today is the only day to attempt any great amd worthy purpose. Opportunity comes to all of us; the diligent ones catch hold of it, the foolish ones let it pass. (Swami Chinmayananda, *We Must*, page 28)

FURTHER READING

- *The Question of Freedom,* Mananam Publication Series, Volume X: Number 2. Piercy, California: Chinmaya Mission West, 1987.
- Swami Chinmayananda, *We Must.* Napa, California: Chinmaya Publications West, 1976. Chapter 8.

Vāsanās 11

Seeing what we've seen about the effects of our innate urges, our *vāsanās*, on our minds and our actions, it becomes clear that *vāsanā* exhaustion must be the main scheme in rendering our minds calm and happy.

Whether our *vāsanās* are coarse or noble, base or fine, if we are being driven by our *vāsanās* we are still not free. If we are bound with chains fashioned of rusted iron or of polished gold, we are bound nevertheless.

Ego-Centered Actions

The third chapter of the *Bhagavad Gītā* presents a method for eliminating *vāsanās* — while we continue living our normal lives of earning a living, going to school, or raising a family. The method of *vāsanā* elimination is simple, so simple that it generally escapes our recognition. In the din of our roaring activities in the workaday world, the onslaught of our immediate demands is so powerful, so incessant, that we have no chance to see the obvious elements of the laws that govern action.

As you'll recall, *vāsanās* are our unmanifest tendencies. Once manifest, they are called our personality, which drives our activities in the world. When our *vāsanās* have become manifest at the thought level, they make themselves known as desires: "I want this" and "I want that." Desires made manifest are our actions. Thus we can say that *vāsanās* in their gross, manifest form create our very lives.

No *vāsanās* — no desires. No desires — no desire-prompted activities. Once we reach that desireless state, we awake to the plane of pure Awareness; we realize our identity with the supreme Reality, our own higher Self. If we set our goal to be the realization of the Self, then our destination is a condition wherein every one of our *vāsanās* is exhausted.

Vāsanās are created during the contact of our body-mind-intellect equipment with the fields of its play in the world. Since we developed our *vāsanās* during these transactions in the world, then it must follow that they can be ended during contacts with that same world — and not by a sudden dash into an isolated cave in the Himalayas.

We may dive under the ocean or move into a mountain cave, but our *vāsanās* will still be with us. And if those *vāsanās* are for drinks or objects of sexual desire or for money or position, if we are anywhere else but in the desolate cave we can at least express them! But in the cave, we can't even do that. So we can only suffer from continued suppression of our urges, and suppression is not the method of reaching spiritual heights. So we will have to exhaust our *vāsanās* where we have developed them. Therefore, all spiritual disciplines provide methods for disciplining our body-mind-intellect equipment in such a way that the existing *vāsanās* get exhausted through our activities and no new *vāsanās* are created.

What the textbooks of Vedanta teach us is this: Whenever we act in the outer world with egocentric desires, the activities leave their footprints in our minds and propel us to repeat the action again and again.

> You have a cup of coffee first thing in the morning, and you have it with the attitude: "I am enjoying it," "I like it," "I want to have it." Then you find yourself growing into the habit of wanting a coffee every morning, then every mid-morning, then after lunch . . .
>
> You have an intoxicating drink, and again you have the "I am enjoying" attitude as you do so. Soon you find yourself

> developing the habit of drinking at every opportunity. Yet, an innocent village woman in a hospital takes brandy as medicine daily for six weeks; but she does not develop the habit of drinking, for she has taken the brandy only for health reasons, not for enjoyment.

An act by itself cannot leave any impression in us, but ego-centered acts, prompted by desire gratification, generate a fresh, new growth of *vāsanās*. When our ego-centered thoughts flow toward a given object or being in a continuous stream, we form an attachment. Thus, all our attachments to the world are forged with our own continuous thoughts.

When this attachment (*saṅga*) increases in its force of flow, it begets the desire (*kāma*) to possess the object of our attachment. When a desire is thwarted, it turns into anger (*krodha*). Anger then gathers in dark chunks to cloud our reason, resulting in delusion (*moha*); under the spell of delusion, we see things as they are not. When we are angry, our perceptions become false, our estimates vague, our judgments wrong, and, therefore, our actions wild and uncontrolled. From this delusion of the mind arises loss of memory, meaning that the storehouse of memories which comprise our knowledge is no longer available to us when the mind is suffused with anger. With the loss of memory, our power of discrimination (*buddhi*) is also lost. Thus, something that started as a simple stream of sensuous thoughts toward an object moved through a terrifying sequence of moods in the mind that resulted in total lack of self-control — and eventually disaster:

> Attachment → desire → anger → delusion → loss of memory → loss of discrimination

In contrast, whenever we undertake an action that is not centered in the ego but is centered in a higher goal, an ideal — thus becoming ideal-centered or God-centered — then our contacts with the outer world become a source for exhausting our *vāsanās*. When the *vāsanās* are exhausted, the mind becomes automatically quiet. And the quieter the mind, the greater the peace and happiness experienced in it. As the *Gītā* says:

> *Therefore, do you always without attachment perform action that should be done, for by performing action without attachment man reaches the Supreme. (Bhagavad Gītā III:19)*

Karma Yoga

This secret of purging our *vāsanās* has been called *karma yoga*, the path of action, in the textbooks of Vedanta. If we fix our vision high and in a spirit of surrender and dedication act in the outer world, the mind becomes purified and the *vāsanās* automatically exhaust themselves. The path of action is a way of life that any one of us can easily adopt. The world around us remaining the same, in whatever condition we may find ourselves, we can grow to unbelievable heights if we can learn to act without selfish, desire-prompted motives (*niṣkāma karma*).

So the message is: "Work. Don't stop working. Continue working, but change your mental attitude. Until now you have been working only for personal gratification. Continue as vigorously as before, but selflessly."

> *But whosoever, controlling the senses by the mind, O Arjuna, engages his organs of action in* karma yoga, *without attachment, he excels. (Bhagavad Gītā III:7)*

The *Gītā* asks us here to control the sense organs (*indriyas*) by the mind. We can achieve this only when we give the mind a brighter and diviner field in which to roam about: a higher goal or ideal. To control the impetuous mind with our sheer will is like attempting to dam a river while it is in flood. When we have learned to control the sense organs somewhat, we have learned to conserve large quantities of energy. Unless this energy is given profitable fields of activity, it is sure to flood the inner world, perhaps even sweep away our personality equilibrium. So the second half of this *Gītā* verse advises us to direct our energies wisely in appropriate fields of activity. The main precaution is: Act without attachment, that is, without egocentric desires.

> When a camera is loaded with a piece of plain white paper, however long we may keep the lenses open against any well-lit object, no impression of the object can mar the white surface of paper. On the other hand, if that very same sheet of paper is sensitized, then even a slight exposure will leave the impression of the object on it.

Similarly, a mind plastered with attachment soon gathers onto itself *vāsanās* during its contacts in its field of activity. So the *Gītā* advises us to act without attachment so that instead of gathering new impressions we may make use of our activities for exhausting our existing *vāsanā*-dirt.

Most of us are egged on to various activities by our search and demand for greater satisfaction and deeper contentment. Satisfaction and contentment are the two wheels of our life-chariot. Goaded by this demand, we earn and save, hoard and spend. However, we seldom find the moments of satisfaction or contentment that we seek. And when they do come, they last only a short while. In contrast, when we dedicate ourselves to selfless work, we gain an ever-increasing amount of inner poise and deep, satisfying calm. When such a calm, single-pointed mind is brought to the meditation seat, the meditator gains the experience of transcending his limited ego. To one who has experienced such egoless bliss, work is no longer training for the mind but a fulfillment of one's own Self-realization. Such a person is the consummate *karma yogi*, blessing humankind with every action he undertakes.

Fruits of Action

The *Gītā* goes on to illuminate the path of *karma yoga* further:

Your right is to work only, but never to its fruits. Let not the fruit of action be your motive, nor let your attachment be to inaction. (Bhagavad Gītā II:47)

Wrong thinking is the bane of life, and all failures in life can be directly traced to impoverished mental equanimity created by unintelligent entertainment of expected fears of possible failure. Many of us refuse to undertake great activities for fear of failure, and even those who dare to undertake challenging endeavors invariably become nervous before they finish them.

Suppose a sales agent has an appointment with an industrial magnate to strike a business deal worth millions of dollars from which he stands to gain a substantial commission. On the day before the appointment, the sales agent allows his mind to indulge in dreams about the size of his commission, followed by fantasies about how he would spend that income by purchasing a house, marrying the woman of his choice, and living happily ever after. When on the appointed hour the agent enters the office of the business magnate, he finds his mental faculties — his alertness, cheerfulness, clarity, and poise — all dried up. His hope for the fruit of his action, that is, his monetary reward, has shackled him with such strong bonds of fear that he trembles at the thought of the deal not going through. Nerves shattered, he proceeds with his appointment, which, of course, cannot end but in dismal failure.

Compare this scene with another:

Another sales agent under the same circumstances ends the meeting in great success, for he is intelligent enough to have rejected any anxiety over the fruits of his labors and therefore has not indulged in futile dreams over them. With his mind at ease, he is jovial, even cheeky, with the business magnate, who is attracted and charmed by the young man's dash and smartness. The bargain is struck with hearty handshakes and pleasant smiles.

If renunciation of attachment to the fruits of our

actions is a guarantee of sure success in the commercial world, how much more so it must be in all the nobler and subtler fields of human endeavor! Rejecting the fruits of our actions, let us act. Let us not waste our potential in worrying over the unborn future. The *Gītā* teaches us to avoid such wasteful expenditure of mental energy and to work instead to the best of our abilities, dedicating our efforts to a noble cause. This is the secret prescription for a work of high inspiration. Such work always ends in brilliant success.

The future is carved out in the present moment. Tomorrow's harvest depends upon today's ploughing and sowing. But if in fear of possible dangers to the crops, the farmer wastes his present chances of ploughing sufficiently and sowing at the right time, it is guaranteed that he will not have any harvest at all to gather in the end. The past is dead; the future is not yet born. If one becomes inefficient in the present, there is no hope for a greater future.

It is interesting to dissect carefully the phrase "fruits of action." In fact, the result of an action, when understood properly, is not anything different from the action itself. An action ends or fulfills itself only in its reaction, and the reaction is simply the action of the present defined in terms of a future moment. Therefore, to worry about the results of our actions is to escape the present and try to live in a future that is not yet born.

The stanza from the *Gītā* gives three injunctions for a *karma yogi*:

1. Be concerned with the action itself.
2. Do not be concerned with the results of your action. Do not entertain the motive of gaining a fixed result (fruit) for a given action.
3. Don't delude yourself into thinking that the above means that you should sit back and do nothing.

In short, *karma yoga* allows us to release ourselves from

our mental preoccupations and thus, through work, to live in joyful self-forgetfulness. The work becomes its own reward. With such a mental approach, we can readily face all of life's challenges, yet remain at peace. And the precious by-product is release from our tormenting *vāsanā* bondages.

A Path for Everyone

The method of *vāsanā* exhaustion called *karma yoga* is expressly well suited to a temperament that is inclined toward action, a typical characteristic of modern man. However, Vedanta allows for many variations in human make-up and prescribes different methods for different temperaments.

Humankind can be typically divided into three main categories:

- **Physically inclined people**. Such people live practically at the level of their sense organs. They are happy when their organs are properly fed and sorrowful when they are starved. They are totally dependent on their environment like any animal. They have little capacity to experience emotional joys or intellectual satisfaction.

- **Emotionally inclined people**. People dwelling in the realm of emotions readily sacrifice their physical needs, since their minds experience a higher quality of joy from emotional satisfaction than from physical gratification. For example, a physical person gets satisfaction out of a sense object only when her own sense organs actually contact it; whereas an emotional person finds greater satisfaction in giving the same object to someone she loves, even though she has the choice to enjoy the object herself.

- **Intellectually inclined people**. These people will readily sacrifice their physical and emotional needs for the sake of an ideal they cherish. By doing so, they enjoy a far superior state of contentment and joy than they would have gained by catering to the other two personalities. The lives of revolutionaries and the joyous sufferings of martyrs are vivid examples.

As our *vāsanās*, so our thoughts; and as our thoughts, so our actions. If we change our thoughts, we change the very timbre of our lives. A change in thoughts can be effected by three methods:

1. By reducing the **quantity** of thoughts
2. By improving the **quality** of thoughts
3. By changing the **direction** of the thought flow

These methods are incorporated in the three well-known yogas: *karma yoga, bhakti yoga,* and *jñāna yoga.*

- **Karma yoga** is the path of action, best suited to active people who have a combined temperament of intellectual plus emotional orientation. This path reduces the **quantity** of thoughts in the mind. The discussions earlier in this chapter illustrate how that approach helps us diminish the load of our *vāsanās*.

- **Bhakti yoga** is the path of devotion, best suited to emotionally tempered people. It helps to improve the **quality** of thoughts entertained. The *bhakta* (a person practicing *bhakti yoga*) spends his emotional energy in singing devotional hymns, praying, or reading the lives of other *bhaktas*, thus changing the quality of thoughts that otherwise might have spent their vitality on romance novels or soap operas.

- **Jñāna yoga** is the path of knowledge, best suited to those of who are predominantly intellectual. When we follow this path, the **direction** of thoughts is changed from the realm of perceptions and emotions to the Life Principle that illumines them all. The *jñānī* (a person practicing *jñāna yoga*) lifts her thoughts from the realm of the physical world — analysis of protein molecules or design of computer software — to the realm of the Spirit, dwelling on the concepts elaborated in the scriptures of the world. She begins asking questions about the meaning of existence: Where did I come from? What happens after death? Is the universe governed by laws?

A fourth path, *hatha yoga*, is also sometimes advised:

- **Hatha yoga** is recommended for those centered in their physical personalities; it prepares them for the other paths.

These varied yogas — or paths, approaches, or techniques — cater to the demands of the entire cross-section of humanity. What the ancient sages prescribed hundreds, even thousands, of years ago, still provides today a broad spectrum of choices to match the inclinations and requirements of modern man.

For Your Study and Reflection

11. Vāsanās

STUDY QUESTIONS, Level 1

1. Explain how selfless action contributes to *vāsanā* exhaustion.

2. In Vedantic terms, what does it mean to say, "Let the work be its own reward"?

3. What path (yoga) do you think your temperament is best suited for? Why? What can you do in your life to set yourself more firmly on this path?

STUDY QUESTIONS, Level 2

1. Explain how, through a chain of inner events, attachment can lead to eventual loss of discrimination.

2. How would you explain the expression "actionless action"?

3. How can even noble *vāsanās* bind us, become impediments on our spiritual path?

FOR YOUR REFLECTION

- When a man thinks of objects, attachment for them arises; from attachment desire is born; from desire arises anger. From anger comes delusion; from delusion, loss of memory; from loss of memory, the destruction of discrimination; from destruction of discrimination, he perishes. (*Bhagavad Gītā* II:62-63)

- Renouncing all actions in Me, with the mind centered on the Self, free from hope and egoism, free from (mental) fever, do you fight! (*Bhagavad Gītā* III:30)

- Thus knowing Him, who is superior to the intellect, and restraining the self by the Self, slay you, O mighty-armed, the enemy in the form of desire, no doubt hard, indeed, to conquer. (*Bhagavad Gītā* III:43)

- But those who worship Me, renouncing all actions in Me, regarding Me as the supreme Goal, meditating on Me with single-minded devotion; for them, whose minds are set on Me, verily I become, ere long, O Partha, the Savior (to save them) from the ocean of finite experiences, *saṁsāra*. (*Bhagavad Gītā* XII:6-7)

FURTHER READING

- *The Holy Geeta* (*Bhagavad Gītā*). Commentary by Swami Chinmayananda. Bombay, India: Central Chinmaya Mission Trust, 1980. Chapter II, verses 62-65, Chapter III.

Guṇas 12

We are essentially divine, but the divinity in us is covered by a veil of thoughts. The differences in the concentration and type of these thoughts give rise to the variety of human beings we see in the world.

Three Thought Textures

The textbooks of Vedanta delineate three thought textures, or *guṇas*, through which the human mind functions:

- *Sattva* = purity: thoughts that are pure and noble
- *Rajas* = passion: thoughts that are passionate and agitated
- *Tamas* = inertia: thoughts that are dull and inactive

These thought textures, in various permutations, determine individual personalities. And on any one day or during any hour of a day, each of us may have one of the three textures play the predominant role:

- Before we fully awaken in the morning, feeling sluggish and sleepy, we are under the influence of the *tāmasic* texture of thought.
- During a busy day at the office, rajas may play a more significant role in defining the texture of our thoughts.

- As we listen to a lecturer talk about the wisdom of the *Bhagavad Gītā*, a *sāttvic* mood may permeate the mind.

Sattva is the subtlest of the three *guṇas*. It is the state of mind filled with equanimity, serenity, and creative poise and therefore best suited for contemplation of the Higher. *Rajas* is the condition of the mind when it is agitated, stormy, ambitious, riddled with overpowering desires, bursting with emotions, and restless with desire-prompted activities. *Tamas* is the state of mind in complete inertia, filled with indolence and carelessness; it describes a condition that reveals no consistency of purpose, amiability of emotions, or nobility in actions.

Each of these thought textures, even *sattva*, is a form of bondage. As the *Bhagavad Gītā* says:

> *"Sattva binds by attachment to happiness and knowledge." (Bhagavad Gītā XIV:6).*

Because a *sāttvic* mind is purified of the agitations of *rajas* and cleansed of the indolence of *tamas*, it allows us to experience a greater share of inner peace and subtler understanding. However, even a *sāttvic* mind is attached to the world of objects-emotions-thoughts and is therefore denied the higher joy of the Self. A golden chain, if sufficiently strong, can also bind us as any iron chain can.

After we have experienced the joys of creative thinking or of the inspiring life of goodness and wisdom, we may get so attached to them that we will sacrifice anything around us in order to consistently experience those subtle joys:

> A scientist working self-dedicatedly in her laboratory; a painter working at his canvas in his drafty studio; a poet unaccepted by society, living in public parks while seeking his own inner joy from his visions and words; martyrs facing cruel persecutions; politicians suffering long years of exile — all experience the joy of living in a *sāttvic* mood.

These are all examples of how people who have experienced the subtler thrills of a *sattva*-soaked mind become bound to their joy-bearing activities, just as much as others may become bound to the thrills of material satisfaction.

When we experience an onslaught of *rājasic* influences in the mind, the mind is choked with a hundred tormenting passions, which express themselves in a variety of urges, desires, and emotions. Once the *rājasic* person fulfills a desire, the next desire is not far behind, robbing him of peace and joy in the mind. The *rājasic* person, always anxious to have more, can never keep quiet but must necessarily act on endlessly, earning and spending and saving and protecting. Either anxious to have more or fearing to lose what he has gained, he is whipped onward from action to action.

Under the influence of *tamas*, our capacity to discriminate between right and wrong is veiled. *Tamas* binds us to our lower nature by providing us with endless misconceptions about the true purpose of life, which leads to a life of indolence and heedlessness. If a person is to leave behind his *tāmasic* life, he must first whip up his *tamas* with *rajas* and then evolve further into *sattva*.

We can summarize the differences between the three *guṇas* thus:

- *Sattva* gives the appearance of seeming inactivity but in reality is characterized by maximum activity; it may be likened to a fan revolving at such a tremendous speed that its motion is not perceptible. A great poet or thinker, absorbed all the time in deep contemplation, is *sāttvic* in nature.
- *Rajas* typifies activity similar to a fan in motion. A passionate youth bristling with activity is *rājasic* in nature.
- Tamas is the quality of mind that can be compared to a motionless fan. An idler who wastes all his time in laziness and sleep is *tāmasic*.

The Caste System

Every human being experiences all three types of thought currents: *sāttvic*, *rājasic*, and *tāmasic*. Only the degree to which any one of these textures predominates determines the type to which an individual belongs.

The four gradations in the caste system of India are nothing but varying degrees of combinations of these thought conditions. The historic misinterpretation and misuse of those gradations comprise what is generally known as the caste system today.

The four castes were originally determined neither by ancestry nor by vocation, but by a person's inner temperament:

- The *brāhmin* (thinker) class is predominantly *sāttvic*, exhibiting only a little *rajas* and minimal traces of *tamas*. The *Gītā* says that this category of people is characterized by serenity, self-restraint, austerity, purity, forgiveness, uprightness, knowledge, and belief in God. Priests, ministers, great thinkers, and subtle poets belong in this category.

- The *kṣatriya* (leader) class exhibits mostly *rājasic* qualities, with a little of *sattva* and *tamas* mixed in. According to the *Gītā*, this category is characterized by prowess, splendor, dexterity, generosity, and lordliness. Leaders of society, such as national presidents or community activists, fall into this category.

- The *vaiṣya* (trader) class has less of *sattva* and *rajas* and more of *tamas*. In this classification fall the traders and business people.

- The *śudra* (laborer) class has a major share of *tamas*, with a little of *rajas* and minimal traces of *sattva*. This category includes people who work on simple and menial tasks, and who are motivated largely by the direction given by others.

Today, these classifications have lost much of their meaning. They have come to designate a hereditary birthright in the society, a mere superficial distinction that divides society into castes. For many years, people have espoused the belief that the four castes are based upon and determined by birth within a given family and by the type of vocation one follows. This confusion arose because the ancient masters of religion, who were also great psychologists, had suggested certain vocations that they thought would be best suited to persons belonging to each respective class of mental and intellectual texture. The intention was merely to guide those who were not well versed in psychology in selecting for themselves a gainful field of work wherein their present mental make-up could be put to best use. However, no rigidity was ordained about this selection. Anyone could pick up or even change one's vocation and transform oneself from a *śudra* to a *vaiṣya* or *kṣatriya* or *brāhmin*, or vice versa. Hindu history is replete with such examples of mental transformation.

As the years rolled by, the basis of classification was forgotten, and people wrongly equated the four grades in the caste system to occupations and birth into families engaged in such occupations. Thus, a priest in a temple is generally considered a *brāhmin,* without any reference to his attainment in study of the scriptures and in practicing the precepts. This is a dismal distortion of the truth. A true *brāhmin* is one who is highly evolved in mind and intellect, has studied and assimilated the scriptural teachings, and daily practices the noble qualities that he has learned. Such a one can be found in any country, religion, or community. He need not be a Hindu or an Indian.

To achieve the mental transformations that catapult us from one classification into another, we have to put forth our own self-effort. A *tāmasic* person has to put in a lot of effort and time to shake off his lethargy and inertia and burst himself into activity before he can even dream of reaching the state of *sattva*. A *rājasic* person is already active, but that activity is directed to acquiring and enjoying the sense objects of the world. The person has to change the direction of her activity to again self-purification instead of sense gratification. The *sāttvic* person is at the portals of Truth. Such a person is fully prepared to take the flight toward Self-realization; she needs only to contemplate and meditate on the supreme Self.

Veils Covering the Self

Each of the thought textures creates a different veil over our true nature, the pure Self. The *Bhagavad Gītā* uses three striking analogies to describe these veilings:

- *Sāttvic desires* veil the Self like **smoke covering the fire.** Even a passing breeze can remove the smoke. Similarly, a little prayer or meditation can remove *sāttvic* desires.
- *Rājasic desires* cover the self like **dust on a mirror**. In this case, some effort is necessary to wipe off the dust. The various religious practices and paths in *vāsanā* exhaustion teach us how to get rid of such desires.
- The pure Self is enveloped in *tāmasic desires* like **a fetus in the womb.** Such desires cannot be removed easily or without much effort. Evolution from this stage involves time and patience, just as a fetus needs to evolve to a fully grown baby to emerge out of the womb.

The three *guṇas* are the expressions of our ignorance of our true nature, the pure Self. One who has "crossed over the *guṇas*," as the *Bhagavad Gītā* says (Chapter XIV), has transcended the mind-intellect equipment and is no longer affected by any mental condition. He lives in the infinite joys of the Self. To him, the ordinary vehicles of joy and sorrow can no longer supply any special quota of experience. Ever steady and balanced, such a Self-realized person lives beyond the storms of the mind, ever peaceful and blissful.

For Your Study and Reflection

12. Guṇas

STUDY QUESTIONS, Level 1

1. Recall the story of Michelangelo throwing pebbles into the pond (Chapter 5, "Action"). What *guṇa* does he exemplify? Explain.

2. Explain how in each of the following verses the listed characteristics (in italics) contribute to the thought texture (*guṇa*) described:

   a. *Passionate, desiring to gain the fruits of action, greedy, harmful, impure, full of delight and grief* — such an agent is said to be *rājasic* (passionate). (*Bhagavad Gītā* XVIII:27)

   b. *Unsteady, vulgar, unbending, cheating, malicious, lazy, despondent,* and *procrastinating* — such an agent is said to be *tāmasic* (dull). (*Bhagavad Gītā* XVIII:28)

3. Explain how *sattva* can be likened to a fan revolving at high speed.

STUDY QUESTIONS, Level 2

1. Is it contradictory to say that you should follow the path of the good, striving to live a good and noble life, yet be

on the lookout that *sattva* may bind you by making you attached to the happiness that results from doing good works? Why or why not?

2. What correspondences do you see between each of the three *guṇas* and the four paths (yogas) described in Chapter 11, "Vāsanās"?

3. Recall from your own experience or from history how a person who was once predominantly characterized by one *guṇa* transformed himself into a person with a subtler *guṇa* texture; for example, a *kṣatriya*-type person becoming a *brāhmin*-type person. What do you think contributed to the transformation?

FOR YOUR REFLECTION

All *Guṇas*

- As fire is enveloped by smoke, as a mirror by dust, as an embryo by the womb, so this is enveloped by that. (*Bhagavad Gītā* III:38)

- The fruit of good action, they say, is *sāttvic* and pure; verily, the fruit of *rajas* is pain; and the fruit of *tamas* is ignorance. (*Bhagavad Gītā* XIV:16)

- The embodied one, having crossed beyond these three *guṇas* out of which the body is evolved, is freed from birth, death, decay, and pain and attains immortality. (*Bhagavad Gītā* XIV:20)

- Better is one's own duty though destitute of merits than the duty of another well performed. He who does the duty ordained by his own nature incurs no sin. (*Bhagavad Gītā* XVIII:47)

Sattva

- An agent who is free from attachment, nonegoistic, endowed with firmness and enthusiasm, and unaffected by success or failure is called *sāttvic* (pure). (*Bhagavad Gītā* XVIII:26)

- Pure *sattva* is like clear water, yet in combination with *rajas* and *tamas*, it provides for transmigration. But when the light of the Self gets reflected in *sattva* alone, then, like the sun, It reveals the entire world of matter. (Shankaracharya, *Vivekacūḍāmaṇi* 117)

Rajas

- That pleasure which arises from contact of the sense organ with the object, which is at first like nectar but in the end like poison, that is declared to be *rājasic* (passionate). (*Bhagavad Gītā* XVIII:38)

- *Rajas* has projecting power. Activity is its very nature. From it, the initial flow of activity has originated. From it, mental modifications such as attachment and grief are also continuously produced. (Shankaracharya, *Vivekacūḍāmaṇi* 111)

Tamas

- The veiling power is the power of *tamas*, which makes things appear to be other than what they actually are. It causes man's repeated transmigration and initiates the action of the projecting power. (Shankaracharya, *Vivekacūḍāmaṇi* 113)

- Darkness, inertness, heedlessness, and delusion — these arise when *tamas* is predominant. (*Bhagavad Gītā* XIV:13)

FURTHER READING

- *The Holy Geeta* (*Bhagavad Gītā*). Commentary by Swami Chinmayananda. Bombay: Central Chinmaya Mission Trust, 1980. Chapter XIV, verses 5-27; Chapter XVIII, verses 19-48.

- Shankaracharya, *Vivekachoodamani* (*Vivekacūḍāmaṇi*). Commentary by Swami Chinmayananda. Bombay: Central Chinmaya Mission Trust, 1987. Verses 111-119.

Sheaths 13

When we first become interested in the spiritual life, we ask questions such as: Where has the world come from? Where will it go? After we gain some understanding of the outer world, we begin inquiring about our private physical world: What is the body? How do the sense organs function?

> To a person born blind, there is no form. To a deaf person, it appears that the cannon is only fuming, not roaring. In order to enjoy tastes and smells, we need a tongue and a nose; in their absence, the world is without taste or smell.

If we take away the five sense organs (*indriyas*), there is no world for us. The world then appears as an existent nothing. We must therefore conclude that our concept of the outer world is gained through our sense organs.

The sense organs cannot function without the mind. We know that in deep sleep the mind does not function, and therefore the sense organs are mute. We then probe further: How does the mind work? From where does our joy bubble forth? Thus, as we continue to probe beyond the gross outer world to the subtler realms of the mind, we move in our contemplative search toward the center deep within, the Self (*Ātman*).

Five Veils for the Self

In Vedanta, each of the external coatings of the Self is called a sheath (*kośa*). Just as the sheath merely encases the blade of a sword, so too the matter coverings appear to encase *Om*, which, in fact, remains untouched by those coverings. Our body forms the grossest covering, the physical sheath. Slightly subtler than the body is the vital-air sheath. Subtler still is the mental sheath (the mind). Still more subtle than the mind is the intellectual sheath; and subtler still is the bliss sheath, the seat of joy.

We can thus delineate five distinct sheaths, called *pañca-kośas* in Sanskrit (literally, "five sheaths"):

1. Food sheath (*annamaya kośa*)
2. Vital-air sheath (*prāṇamaya kośa*)
3. Mental sheath (*manomaya kośa*)
4. Intellectual sheath (*vijñānamaya kośa*)
5. Bliss sheath (*ānandamaya kośa*)

The Food Sheath

The physical body, the outermost precincts of our personality, beyond which we do not physically exist, is called the food sheath. It is so called because it has emerged from the essence of the food assimilated by the father; it is nourished in the womb by the food eaten by the mother; it continues to exist because of food eaten by the individual; and, ultimately, after death, it goes back to fertilize the earth and becomes food for worms and plants. This physical structure, arising out of food, existing in food, and going back to become food, is appropriately called the food sheath.

The food sheath consists of the five organs of perception (*jñāna indriyas*) and the five organs of action (*karma indriyas*).

The five organs of perception (*jñāna indriyas*) are:

1. Eyes
2. Ears
3. Nose
4. Tongue
5. Skin

The five organs of action (*karma indriyas*) are:

1. Hands
2. Legs
3. Organ of speech
4. Genital organ
5. Organs of evacuation

The five organs of perception are apertures in the body through which stimuli from the external world, in the form of color, form, sound, smell, taste, and touch, enter the physical body. These stimuli react on the inner equipment, the mind-intellect, which issues responses. These responses are expressed by the organs of action.

The Vital-Air Sheath

The five-fold faculties (*pañca-prāṇas*), which correspond to the five physiological systems detailed by physiologists, represent the vital-air sheath. The five faculties (*prāṇas*) that comprise this sheath are:

1. Faculty of perception (*prāṇa*): Controls the fivefold perceptions of seeing, hearing, smelling, tasting, and touching.
2. Faculty of excretion (*apāna*): Controls the throwing out or rejecting by the body of excreta such as feces, urine, sperm, sputum, and perspiration.
3. Faculty of digestion (*samāna*): Digests the food received by the stomach.
4. Faculty of circulation (*vyāna*): Distributes the digested food to various parts of the body through the blood stream.
5. Faculty of thinking (*udāna*): Capacity to entertain, absorb, and assimilate new thoughts. This capacity helps us to acquire new knowledge and to educate ourselves.

We need to distinguish the faculty of thinking (*udāna*) from the intellect (*buddhi*), which is our faculty of discrimination. *Udāna* is the capacity to acquire new knowledge, while *buddhi* is the faculty of discriminating against the background of knowledge already possessed. Against the light of background knowledge, the intellect judges between pairs of opposites — good and bad, right and wrong. As a person advances in age, he gradually loses his faculty of thinking (*udāna*); however, he very likely attains a sharper intellect (*buddhi*). We can explain the former deficiency by aging of the instruments of thinking, while the latter gain in intellectual capacity results from an accumulation of a reservoir of knowledge on which the individual can draw in making decisions.

The vital-air functions are manifest as long as the person is breathing air. They are therefore together called the vital-air sheath. The vital-air sheath controls and regulates the food sheath, which we can see when the physical body becomes adversely affected when the *prāṇas* are not functioning properly. Physiological activities determine the health and beauty of the anatomical structure, and as a person advances in age, the five faculties gradually become weaker.

The Mental and Intellectual Sheaths

The mental sheath regulates and orders the vital-air sheath. For example, when the mind is upset, the functions of the *prāṇas,* and therefore of the physical body, are affected. When the mind is joyous, both the vital-air sheath and the physical sheath work to optimum efficiency. The intellectual sheath, still subtler, controls the mental sheath.

Let's elaborate further on the differentiation between the mind and the intellect that we analyzed earlier:[1]

[1] In Chapter 9, "Mind."

1. The mind receives external stimuli through the sense organs. The intellect, being the discriminating faculty, examines and judges the stimuli received by the mind and communicates back to the mind its decision on the type of directives to be sent to the organs of action.

> An individual touches a hotplate. On contact, he quickly withdraws his hand. But before he does that, a series of reactions take place imperceptibly: As soon as the finger comes in contact with the heat, the skin carries the stimulus of heat to the mind, which, in turn, puts it up to the intellect. The intellect, which has a storehouse of memories of past experience and knowledge, concludes on the basis of such knowledge that the object contacted is dangerous, and it therefore orders the mind to withdraw the hand. The mind, in turn, communicates the order to the respective muscles of the body.

2. The mind is a continuous flow of thoughts. If each thought is likened to a pail of water, then the mind can be likened to a river, which is nothing but a flow of water. A pail of water has no power of its own, but when many pails of water together flow in continuous motion, they develop dynamism and strength. Similarly, when thoughts flow continuously, they create an apparent power and strength — called the mind.

The direction of a river is determined by its banks. If the banks turn to the left, the water in the river turns to the left. In the same way, the human intellect sets the direction of the thought flow. If a person's intellect is noble, the thoughts flowing in the mind must necessarily be noble also. If, however, the intellect is base and vulgar, the mind follows suit.

3. The mind is the seat of emotions such as love, greed, hatred, compassion, and jealousy. The intellect, in contrast, is the springboard of all ideas and ideologies, such as freedom, liberty, political theories, and mathematical formulas.

4. The mind can function only in known realms, whereas the intellect can reach into yet unchartered realms of thought.

5. The mind is ever in a state of flux. It vacillates to and fro. When the thoughts stabilize themselves to form a willed judgment, we have the function called the intellect.

> When Ramesh is indecisive about eating vegetarian or nonvegetarian food, his thoughts are in a condition of doubt and indecision; this is the function of the mind. But when he takes a firm decision to become a vegetarian, his thoughts reflect the status of the intellect.

Therefore, what the mind is at one moment becomes the intellect at another moment; and, conversely, the intellect can be reduced to the status of the mind when its decisions are broken by another powerful intellect. This kind of changing between mind and intellect is possible because the differences between the mind and intellect are purely functional. We do not have two separate organs called the mind and the intellect. The mind and intellect have only functions, but no structure. In essence, both of them consist of thoughts.

The Bliss Sheath

The bliss sheath is the innermost of the five sheaths and therefore the most subtle. It consists exclusively of *vāsanās*, our innate tendencies, before their grossification into thoughts and actions. The bliss sheath is experienced in the state of deep sleep, a state in which there is no manifestation other than complete, unadulterated ignorance ("I know nothing").

This innermost of sheaths is described by the word *bliss* because when we are associated with it, as in deep sleep, we experience relative bliss. In the waking state and dream state, we experience incessant agitations, but once we reach the chamber of dreamless sleep, whether we are rich or poor, healthy or sick, young or old, we experience an undisturbed peace. In that state we are blissful because the usual agitations we experience in the waking or dream states have stopped totally. However, this relative bliss is not the same as the infinite bliss of God-realization.

The textbooks of Vedanta use the following terms to describe the realm of unmanifest tendencies:

- Bliss sheath
- *Vāsanās*
- Ignorance (of the pure Self)
- Nonapprehension (of the supreme Reality)[2]
- Causal body[3]
- State of deep sleep

Because these terms are so prevalent in Vedantic literature, knowledge of them becomes essential to our study. Although in essence they are the same, each is used to indicate a particular aspect of the same thing.

Transcending the Sheaths

Beyond the five sheaths is *Om*, the Self (*Ātman*), the core of the five-sheathed structure. The five sheaths are like five layers of dress worn by the Self, each of which is totally different from the wearer.

We say that the vital-air sheath is *within* the food sheath, and that the mental sheath is *within* the vital-air sheath, and so on; and that the Self is innermost. Such a description may give us the idea that the Self is something very minute, located inside layers and layers of matter. Yet, the Upanishads describe the Self as all-pervading. Therefore, the term *within* has to be understood in a special philosophical context. When we say that a sheath is *within* another, we mean that the inner one is subtler than the outer one. The subtler controls and feeds the grosser. The Self, the subtlest of all, is the controller and nourisher of all the five layers.

Again, the subtlety of something is measured by its pervasiveness.

---

[2] To be discussed in Chapter 16, "Māyā."

[3] To be discussed in Chapter 14, "Three Worlds."

> When a piece of ice melts, the water formed occupies a larger area, and hence in philosophy we would say that water is subtler than ice. When the water is boiled, the steam generated spreads through the entire atmosphere, thereby filling a much greater space than the water did. Steam is therefore considered subtler than water.

Similarly, the food sheath is considered the most gross because it is least pervasive. The vital-air, mental, and intellectual sheaths follow the ascending order of subtlety. The bliss sheath, being the most pervasive, is the subtlest of the five sheaths. And the Self is even more subtle than the bliss sheath.

- The food sheath is the grossest level, as the dimensions of the body remain almost the same at all times. At best, the body may expand by a few inches around the waistline after a heavy meal.
- The perceptions, part of the vital-air sheath, go beyond the boundaries of the physical body. The sense organs perceive forms, sounds, smells, tastes, and touches that lie beyond the boundaries of the physical structure.
- The mental sheath is more pervasive than the vital-air sheath, since the mind can comprehend within its orbit everything that is already known, even though those fields of knowledge may stretch beyond the scope of physical perception. Thus, while perceptions are confined to the perceiving limits of the sense organs, the mind can contact distant realms.
- The intellectual sheath extends even farther than the mental sheath, since it has the capacity to travel beyond known realms to new, unknown areas of thought.
- The bliss sheath is most pervasive. Consisting of *vāsanās*, the bliss sheath is the subtlest of the five layers, since it controls the behavior of all the above four layers. *Vāsanās* are the cause of the other sheaths, and as the cause they are

inherent in the effect.[4] Besides inherently existing in the four sheaths, *vāsanās* remain in their unmanifest form in the state of deep sleep. None of the other sheaths has access to the bliss sheath.

- The Self pervades all the sheaths. It is infinite and all-pervading. The subtlety of the Self is absolute and beyond human comprehension.

The goal of life is to transcend the five sheaths and learn to identify with the pure, limitless, all-pervading Self — that subtle repository of joy and peace over which the sheaths have thrown a temporary veil.

[4] See the discussion on cause and effect in Chapter 10, "Karma."

For Your Study and Reflection

13. Sheaths

STUDY QUESTIONS, Level 1

1. Imagine what the world would be like if you had the hearing ability of a dog and the sensing ability of a bat. What does this tell you about the absolute or relative nature of the external world?

2. Explain at least three differences between the mind and the intellect.

3. Describe an example from your own experience of how the mental function of your thoughts (mind) was in conflict with the intellectual function (intellect).

STUDY QUESTIONS, Level 2

1. Current thinking puts much emphasis on the relationship of the body and the mind in maintaining good health. Give examples of studies you have heard about. How do these correlate with the idea that the subtler layers (mind-intellect) influence the more gross sheaths (vital-air and physical sheaths)?

2. Explain, from the Vedantic perspective, why dreamless sleep is blissful.

3. How can you reconcile the fact that the scriptures describe the pure Self both as "innermost" and as "all-pervading"?

FOR YOUR REFLECTION

- The body is a product of food. It constitutes the food sheath. It exists because of food and dies without it. It is a bundle of skin, flesh, blood, bones, and filth. Never can it be the self-existing, the eternally pure Self. (Shankaracharya, *Vivekacūḍāmaṇi* 154)

- The vital-air sheath cannot be the Self because it is a modification of air. Like air it enters the body and goes out of it, never knowing its joys or sorrows or those of others. It is ever dependent upon the Self. (Shankaracharya, *Vivekacūḍāmaṇi* 166)

- Covered by the five sheaths, such as the food sheath, which are produced by its own divine power, the Self ceases to appear, just as the water in a tank ceases to appear due to the collection of moss, which is born out of itself (water). When the moss is removed, absolutely pure water, which can quench pangs of thirst and give immediate joy, becomes visible. When all the five sheaths have been negated, the Self is apprehended as being the essence of everlasting bliss, as the indwelling, self-effulgent supreme Spirit. (Shankaracharya, *Vivekacūḍāmaṇi* 149-151)

FURTHER READING

- Shankaracharya, *Vivekachoodamani* (*Vivekacūḍāmaṇi*). Commentary by Swami Chinmayananda. Bombay: Central Chinmaya Mission Trust, 1987. Verses 154-188.

Three Worlds 14

As we have already seen,[1] the five sheaths are like five layers of clothing over the innermost Spirit, the pure Self. We can also view the sheaths as comprising three bodies that envelop the Self.

Three Bodies

The Gross Body

The food and vital-air sheaths together constitute the gross body.[2] The gross body contains the five organs of perception (eyes, ears, nose, tongue, and skin), the five organs of action (hands, legs, organ of speech, genital organ, and organs of excretion), and the five physiological faculties called *prāṇas*.

---

[1] In Chapter 13, "Sheaths."

[2] In some texts of Vedanta, the gross and subtle bodies are categorized differently, namely, the mind, the intellect, the organs of perception, the organs of action, and the vital-air sheath are all considered as part of the subtle body. The seeming discrepancy is easily resolved: The vital-air sheath is, as it were, a glue that holds the subtle body to the gross. At death, the vital-air sheath can be considered as part of either the gross or the subtle body.

When the organs of perception and the organs of action are categorized with the subtle body, we can think of them not as the physical organs, but the power behind those organs, such as "the power of vision," which, in essence, is located in the mind-intellect equipment. If the mind does not come in contact with the sense organs, no perception is possible.

The gross body is the medium through which we contact the outer world of objects and gather stimuli for our experiences of joy and sorrow. When the pure Self identifies with the gross body, It manifests Itself as **the waker.** The waker's field of experience is the waking world.

The Subtle Body

The mental and intellectual sheaths together form the subtle body, which is made up exclusively of thoughts. However, those thoughts exhibit functional differences. In addition to the two functions we've already looked at — mind and intellect — we now add another two, *ahaṅkāra* and *citta*:

1. Mind (*manas*)
2. Intellect (*buddhi*)
3. Ego (*ahaṅkāra*)
4. Illuminating aspect; conditioned consciousness (*citta*)

The four functions that constitute the subtle body are our inner equipment (*antaḥkaraṇa*) — as contrasted with the outer equipment residing in the gross body.

The four components of the subtle body are merely functional designations, not separate organs. Organs have both structure and function; however, these four have no structure, but function only.

1. *Mind.* When a stimulus from the external world first enters us through the organs of perception, it causes a disturbance in thought. Thoughts in this condition of disturbance are called the mind.

2. *Intellect.* After the first impact is over, the disturbance dies down, and our thoughts come to a decision. Thoughts in this condition of decision are called the intellect.

3. *Ego.* A disturbance and a decision are related to each other only if they belong to a single individual. When both of them reside in a person, she is aware that the disturbance and the decision are hers. The awareness that an individual possesses a given thought, such as a decision, is yet another

thought, and its functional name is ego. Simply said, it is a feeling of "I-ness" and "my-ness."

The ego exists in reference to the past. A sense of ego develops in us on a foundation built of memories of certain facts of life already experienced:

- I am the daughter of so-and-so.
- I was educated at such-and-such.
- I loved, hated, won, lost, and so on.

In short, we are the sum total of all of our retained memories of our experiences in the past. That "I" concept also includes our hopes for the future.

4. *Illuminating aspect; conditioned consciousness (citta). Citta* is the illuminating aspect in our thoughts that makes us aware of the other three functions. Through this function, we become aware of our mind and intellect and know that any thought we entertain is our own.

Pure Consciousness is unconditioned by any type of human equipment. However, when pure Consciousness functions through the mind, the intellect, and the ego, it becomes *as though* conditioned by these types of equipment. This "conditioned consciousness" is called *citta*. When the conditioning is eliminated, the conditioned consciousness merges back into pure Consciousness.

> A room is filled with sunlight. Outside the room, all-pervading sunlight shines in every direction. Within the room, it is conditioned by the walls of the room. As long as the walls exist, the sunlight in it *apparently* remains conditioned by them. When the walls are removed, conditioned sunlight within the room merges with the total sunlight.

When the pure Self (or pure Consciousness) identifies with the subtle body, It manifests Itself as **the dreamer.** The dreamer's field of experience is the dream world, that world which we all participate in while dreaming.

The Causal Body

The bliss sheath is called the causal body. It consists of *vāsanās* in their unmanifest form. When in deep sleep both the gross and the subtle bodies are inactive, the causal body prevails. In this condition the worlds of waking and dream are obliterated, but the vision of the pure Self is not yet available. It is a state of nonapprehension. In this state, we know neither the higher Reality nor the lower plurality. It is a state of utter ignorance. When pure Consciousness identifies Itself with the causal body, It manifests Itself as **the deep sleeper,** who goes through a homogeneous experience of nothingness (complete ignorance).

Three States

Although our true nature is pure Consciousness, we pass through the three different states of waker, dreamer, and deep sleeper as a result of the play of Consciousness in the gross, subtle, and causal bodies, respectively.

When the identification with these three bodies or three states falls away, we apprehend the pure nature of the Self, the all-pervading, unlimited Consciousness. In that state, which transcends the states of waking, dreaming, and sleeping, we become Self-realized.

> A single entity expressing itself as many has a parallel in our daily lives. Each of us plays different roles in life. At home we acquire the status of a child relative to our parents or of a father or mother relative to our children; in the office, we assume the position of a worker or a manager; at school, we play the role of a student; on the tennis court, we become a tennis player. The child, father, mother, worker, student, and tennis player have no existence independent of the individual.

The Self is one and the same in all human beings, regardless of their nationality, caste, or creed. The nature of the pure Self is absolute bliss. This being so, we constantly endeavor to regain our real nature of bliss by trying to gain

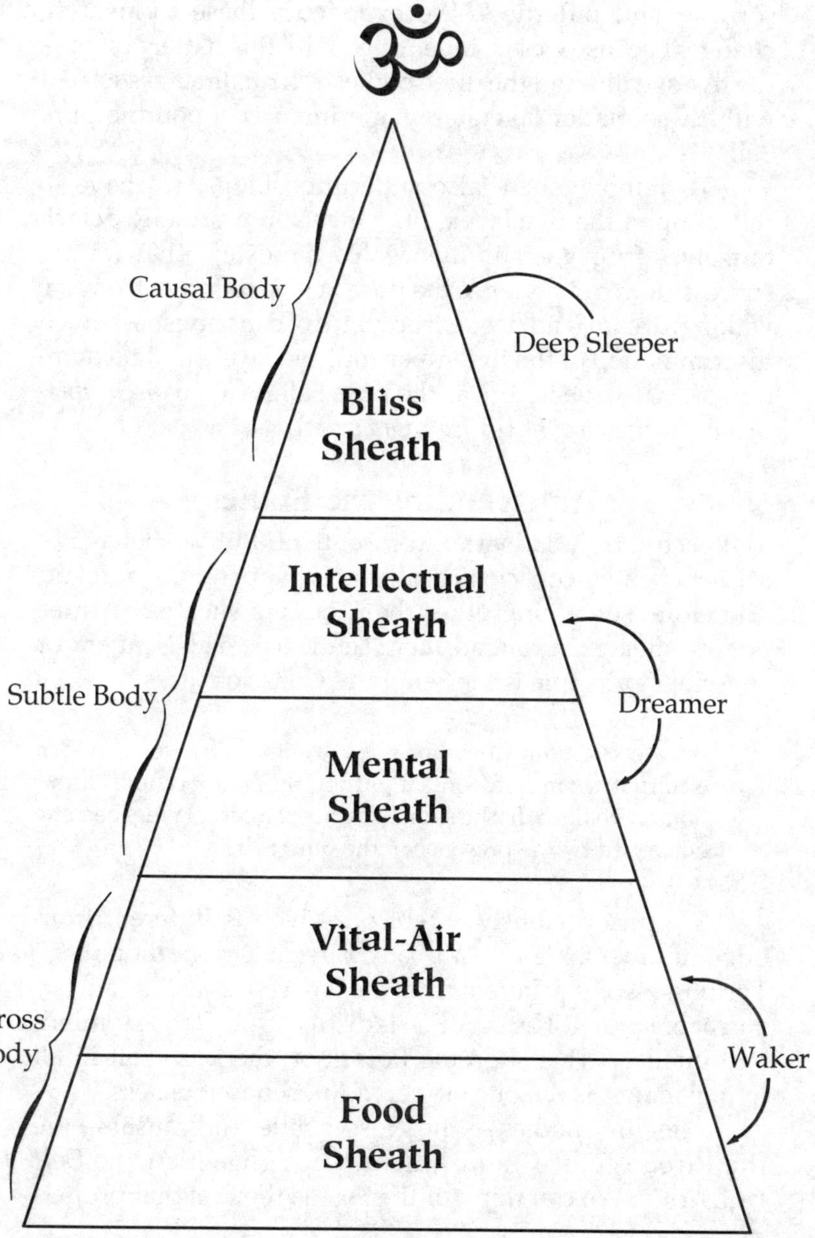

Causal Body
Deep Sleeper
Bliss Sheath
Intellectual Sheath
Subtle Body
Dreamer
Mental Sheath
Vital-Air Sheath
Gross Body
Waker
Food Sheath

more and more happiness from the world. While we thus struggle, we obtain short spasms of joy, soon followed by sorrows and bitterness. We experience these tormenting changes because we have identified with the matter layers — the five sheaths and the three bodies. All qualities associated with these matter layers are superimposed upon the pure Self.

To remove such false superimpositions, we have to reflect upon the five layers of matter and gradually detach ourselves from their influence. To the extent that we are successful, we experience the pure Self as different from the waking, dream, and deep-sleep states of consciousness. Such discrimination of the five superimposed layers and recognition of one's true nature as the pure Self is called *discrimination of the five sheaths* (*pañca kośa viveka*).

Transcending the Bodies

Matter, by itself, is inert and insentient. But we behave as sentient beings, conscious of all that is happening around us. Therefore, something other than the five sheaths or three bodies must exist to lend them sentience. This sentient or conscious principle is the Self, pure Consciousness.

> An electric bulb does not glow by itself. However, when electricity comes in contact with it, the bulb becomes luminous with light. In the same way, inert matter layers become enlivened by the presence of the pure Self.

We unconsciously accept ourselves as different from our equipment. We say: "*My* body, *my* emotions, *my* thoughts." The possessor is different from the possessed, just as I am not *my* car or *my* dog. The pure Self is distinct from *Its* body, mind, and intellect. This supreme Possessor, the pure Self in all living beings, is the one all-pervading Consciousness.

The three bodies — the gross, subtle, and causal — are the three types of equipment through which the Self functions. We can think of the Self as the fuel that propels these three vehicles to perform. The Self is the life force that functions through the three bodies to create the human personality — the waker-dreamer-sleeper.

Because pure Consciousness is that which makes our physical and mental equipment function, we cannot use the intellect to see Consciousness directly, just as the eye cannot see itself.

> *A lighted lamp does not need another lamp to illumine its light. So too,* Ātman, *which is Knowledge itself, needs no other knowledge to know It.* (Shankaracharya, *Ātma Bodha* 29)

Since pure Consciousness falls beyond the scope of our mental equipment, our mind projects a false interpretation upon Reality. It then identifies with this misinterpretation and experiences the pluralistic world. This phenomenon of projecting and identifying is called *superimposition*.

The causal body arises out of our ignorance (*avidyā*) of Reality. Comprised of our unmanifest *vāsanās*, it is the very *cause* of our world of plurality. That world of plurality is nothing but a false projection arising from our ignorance of Reality.

> Sheela has joined a large get-together at her friend's house. She has just finished talking to two of her friends and wanders off to get some more food at the snack table. As she's biting into a samosa, she looks over at the two friends and sees them looking in her direction, laughing and talking. She begins to suspect that they're talking about her and starts building up stories in her imagination about what they may be saying. Out of her ignorance of what is really going on rises a misapprehension, her imagined version of reality.

To move beyond the false projection, the pluralistic world, and realize the Self is to transcend the three bodies. But many of us try to clutch onto the three bodies — while trying to reach toward a higher state of bliss.

> A tin contains an assortment of chocolates of different types, shapes, and colors, all wrapped beautifully in colored foil. In his ignorance, a child chews the chocolate along with the colorful wrappings. No doubt he enjoys the sweetness, but the enjoyment is followed by stomach pains caused by the swallowed foil.

So too, the Self, the embodiment of absolute bliss, is wrapped in layers of matter and labeled variously: *brāhmin*, *śudra*, American, Hindu, Muslim, Eskimo, woman, man, European, Australian. We, the children of absolute bliss, try to enjoy the sweetness of the bliss along with the wrappings. We experience a few flickers of joy, to be sure, but they are soon followed by sorrow. The only solution is: Analyze and discard the five layers of matter wrappings and realize the Self as different from the waker, dreamer, and deep sleeper.

Macrocosm

Consciousness, the enlivener of the individual human being, is the same Consciousness that acts as the substratum for the entire cosmos. In short, the substratum of the microcosm, the individual (*jīva*), is the same as the substratum of the macrocosm, the universe (*jagat*). In the case of the individual, the substratum is called the Self, or *Ātman*, and in the case of the macrocosm it is called the supreme Reality, or *Brahman*.

- Consciousness functioning through the aggregate of all gross bodies is called the cosmic form of the waker (*Virāt*).
- Consciousness functioning through the aggregate of all subtle bodies (all minds and intellects) is called the Creator (*Hiraṇyagarbha*), the cosmic form of the dreamer.
- Consciousness functioning through the aggregate of all causal bodies (total *vāsanās*, also known as *māyā*, or total ignorance of the Self) is called *Īśvara*, the cosmic form of the deep sleeper.[3]

[3] *Māyā* will be discussed in greater detail in Chapter 16, "Māyā."

MICROCOSM

Consciousness functioning through

↓

The gross body = The waker

The subtle body = The dreamer

The causal body = The deep sleeper

MACROCOSM

Consciousness functioning through

↓

Total gross bodies = Virāt

Total subtle bodies = Hiraṇyagarbha

Total causal bodies = Īśvara

The combination of the cosmic waker, cosmic dreamer, and cosmic deep sleeper constitutes the cosmos, the macrocosm.

The *vāsanās* in a person are the cause for his mind-intellect, which in turn are the cause for his gross body. Similarly, the total *vāsanās* (*māyā*) produce the total mind-intellect (*Hiraṇyagarbha*), which creates the total universe (*Virāt*). *Māyā* is therefore considered the root cause of the universe.

As you'll recall,[4] the individual (*jīva*) is comprised of the perceiver-feeler-thinker (PFT). The sum total of all the *jīvas* in the world is the concept of God, the Lord, *Īśvara*. This *Īśvara* is the God-Principle, not the individual gods or deities of Hinduism, such as Rama, Krishna, or Shiva. The particular incarnations (*avatāras*), such as Krishna, are manifestations of the God-Principle.

The relationship that exists among *jīva*, *jagat*, and *Īśvara* is explained by the following example:

> A piece of cloth has some decorative patterns woven into it by the same thread of which the cloth is made. The various patterns together form an image of a flower garden. The total concept we gain — that is, of a flower garden — is similar to our total concept of the world (*jagat*), with its oceans, continents, and mountains.
>
> Now, in what does this piece of cloth exist? Does it have an existence apart from the thread? If we were to remove all the threads, where would be the cloth? The cloth *is* the thread, but when we don't see the thread but only the patterns fashioned of it, we accept the concept of a flower garden.
>
> The thread is a symbol for the God-Principle, *Īśvara*. The individual decorative patterns symbolize the individual beings (*jīvas*). The totality of patterns, an image of a flower garden, is our total world (*jagat*).
>
> What is the essence of the flower garden? It is nothing but the thread. Except for the thread, there would have been no

[4] From Chapter 5, "BMI."

pattern. Similarly, but for the God-Principle, *Īśvara*, there would have been no world.

Thus, varied names and forms (*nāmarūpa*) constitute the total concept of the world as we see it, but in essence the world is nothing but a pattern fashioned of the essential stuff, the God-Principle. If we take away the divine Principle, the entire pattern must necessarily perish, just as the piece of cloth ends when all the threads in it are removed.

Now, let us analyze the God-Principle one step deeper, again using the thread-cloth analogy:

> What is the thread made of? Is the thread a self-born thing? Does it exist of itself?
>
> What is the cause of the thread? From the standpoint of the cloth, the thread is the cause. But is the thread its own cause? If it has a cause, what is its cause? Its cause is cotton.
>
> But for the cotton, the thread would not exist; but for the thread, neither the cloth nor the patterns would exist. In cotton, all the three — thread, cloth, and patterns — exist. And into cotton all three must go when thread, cloth, and patterns are destroyed.

The relationship between the individual ego and God is the relationship between the pattern and the thread. God is the immediate transformation of the permanent Truth, the supreme Reality, and the next transformation down is the human being.

Individual pattern	=	*jīva*
Image of a flower garden	=	*jagat*
Thread	=	God-Principle *(Īśvara)*
Cotton	=	Supreme Reality *(Brahman)*

According to Vedanta, the supreme Reality (*Brahman*) undergoes no modification, just as the cotton always remains cotton:

> We give cotton various names according to the form it takes: We give it the name *thread* at one stage and the name *cloth* at another. According to our changing perspective, the same piece of cloth changes its impression on us. On a casual look, we see it as a piece of cloth. When we observe it more closely, we see the threads that constitute it. When we examine it closer still, we have the "vision" of the cotton of which the thread is made. Having once seen the cotton, we no longer see the difference between the many and various patterns, nor between the different kinds of cloth.

In the same way, once we have the vision of the underlying Reality of things, no change in name and form can take away from that understanding. The plurality of names and forms merges into the one Reality, the substratum of them all.

Nothing new is ever created by anyone. A change in name and form is all that creation means. Creation is reconversion. In creating a thing, three essential factors are necessary, which, in aggregate, are called the *cause*. The three factors are, as they apply to a potter's creation of a vase from clay:

1. The raw material, the *material cause* for the creation: clay
2. The *instrumental cause*, the equipment used in the creation: the potter's wheel
3. The *efficient cause*, the intelligence behind the creation: the potter

In all vase creations in the world, the potter is separate from the clay. However, in the creative process of the finite emerging from the Infinite, the material cause and the efficient cause are one and the same. Just as bubbles in water are but water rising in water, existing in water, and then merging back into water once the bubbles burst, so too the plurality of the world is but a play of names and forms upon the supreme Reality, *Brahman*.

The relationship between the microcosm and the macrocosm varies according to the individual personality. A person with a huge load of *vāsanās* imagines a big gulf between the microcosm (himself) and the macrocosm (the world or the universe). To him, the individual and the cosmos are poles apart. But as the individual cleanses himself of his *vāsanās* and thereby reduces his ego-driven concepts of "I-ness" and "my-ness," he finds his individuality blending harmoniously with the world around him. In the final stages of evolution, when the ego is completely annihilated, the person recognizes a perfect oneness between the individual and the cosmos. Only the one Reality remains.

For Your Study and Reflection

14. Three Worlds

STUDY QUESTIONS, Level 1

1. Explain how our sense of ego is related to our memories, to what has happened to us in the past.

2. Explain how identification with the various matter layers takes us further away from happiness.

3. Why can't we perceive Consciousness directly with our intellect? How does this inability lead to the phenomenon called *superimposition*?

STUDY QUESTIONS, Level 2

1. Give an example from your own experience of how ignorance of a thing or a situation became the cause of projection.

2. Explain the relationship of *jīva* (the individual), *jagat* (the world), and *Īśvara* (the God-Principle). Use an analogy, if appropriate.

3. How do names and forms define our world?

FOR YOUR REFLECTION

- The world appears to be true so long as *Brahman*, the substratum, the basis of all this creation, is not realized. It is like the illusion of silver in the mother of pearl. (Shankaracharya, *Ātma Bodha* 7)

- All-pervading space appears to be diverse on account of its association with various conditionings, which are different from each other. Space becomes one on the destruction of these limiting adjuncts. So also the omnipresent Truth appears to be diverse on account of Its association with the various conditionings and becomes One on the destruction of the conditionings. (Shankaracharya, *Ātma Bodha* 10)

- In its identification with the five sheaths, the immaculate Self appears to have borrowed their qualities upon Itself — as is the case of a crystal that appears to gather unto itself the color of its vicinity (blue cloth, etc.). Through discriminating self-analysis and logical thinking, one should separate the pure Self within from the sheaths, just as one separates the rice from the husk, bran, etc., that are covering it. (Shankaracharya, *Ātma Bodha* 15-16)

- Attachment, desire, pleasure, pain, etc., are perceived to exist so long as the mind functions. They are not perceived in deep sleep when the mind ceases to exist. Therefore, they belong to the mind alone and not to the Self. (Shankaracharya, *Ātma Bodha* 23)

- The body, etc., up to the causal body, which are objects perceived, are as perishable as bubbles. Realize through discrimination that I am the pure *Brahman*, ever completely separate from all these. (Shankaracharya, *Ātma Bodha* 31)

FURTHER READING

- Shankaracharya, *Ātma Bodha*. Commentary by Swami Chinmayananda. Bombay: Central Chinmaya Mission Trust, 1987.

Vedanta 15

The scriptures tell us that our real nature is pure knowledge and pure bliss. But our sense of ego has created a grievous misunderstanding that we are ego-bound, limited beings. Whether we know it or not, through a slow process of evolution, all of us are creeping toward this goal of Self-realization every hour of our days. Life's experiences are wearing us down in a slow mill of sorrow — only to make us sit up and realize the foolish delusion in which we are suffering. Therefore, the cry of all religions of the world is:

Wake up! Arise! Stop not until the goal is reached!

Vedanta is the subjective science that shows us how to reach that sacred goal and reveals to us our own true nature. That subtle science arose from an oral tradition in India thousands of years ago. The valleys and forests of the great Himalayas and the waters of the mighty Ganges kindled in many inspired and sensitive hearts a hunger to know the mysteries of the power that quickens inert matter into conscious beings. The reflections of these masters became the scriptures we know today.

The Vedas

The wisdom of those ancient sages — called *brahmavidyā* in Sanskrit, "knowledge of *Brahman*" — was communicated from teacher to taught by word of mouth, bringing about the traditional preceptor-disciple lineage (*guru-śiṣya-paramparā*) in India. In those days of pure oral transmission of the immortal truths of Vedanta, every verse of scriptural wisdom was composed in the mouth of the guru and printed directly on the memory slabs of his disciples' minds. Then, some thousands of years before Christ, the great poet-sage Veda Vyasa compiled and codified the entire scriptural wealth into four books:[1]

- *Ṛg Veda*
- *Yajur Veda*
- *Sāma Veda*
- *Atharva Veda*

The Vedas were not the product of any one individual, but were the inspired declarations of a number of rishis over many generations. These great masters, absorbed as they were in a state transcending all attitudes of "I" and "mine," did not even append their names to these holy texts.

Of the numerous and different sets of *śāstras* (scriptures), the most ancient are the Vedas. All other *śāstras* originated from them. The word *Veda* is derived from the Sanskrit root *vid*, "to know." Thus, *Veda* came to mean "knowledge of the Truth." Just as God and the creation are infinite and eternal, so also Veda, or knowledge of God, is infinite and exists eternally in the universe.

Each of the four Vedas is divided into four main sections:

- *Mantras* — Lyrical chants adoring the beauty of nature
- *Brāhmaṇas* — Elaborate descriptions of rituals
- *Āraṇyakas* — Prescriptions for various methods of subjective worship (*upāsanas*)
- *Upaniṣads*[2] — Declarations of the highest spiritual truths

[1] The exact time of the origin of the Vedas is still under debate. Recent research points to the time of the Vedas as being at least 4,000 B.C., considerably earlier than previously thought.

[2] *Upaniṣad*, with a diacritical mark under the ṣ, is the direct transliteration from the Sanskrit; the anglicized version of the word is Upanishad.

The Upanishads constitute the concluding portion of each of the four Vedas. The aggregate content of all these Upanishads is called Vedanta:

• *veda*	=	"knowledge"
• *anta*	=	"the end"
• *Vedānta*	=	"the end portion of the Vedas"
		"the end (or the goal) of knowledge"
		"the most profound knowledge"

These end portions of the Vedas — the body of knowledge called Vedanta — rationally explain the supreme Reality and the means for attaining Self-realization. The Upanishads are also known as *Śruti* ("that which is heard," again underscoring the oral tradition of the transmission of knowledge from teacher to taught).

Besides the *Śruti*, the religious literature of India also includes:[3]

- *Smṛtis*. Auxiliary scriptures that explain the *Śruti*. Manu, Yajnavalkya, and other great thinkers contributed to this body of traditional law composed for the guidance of people's daily lives. The *Smṛtis* include codes of social, ethical, moral, and domestic laws of conduct. They also describe ceremonies and rites connected with the domestic life of the Hindus.

- *Itihāsas*. Histories, including epics such as the *Mahābhārata* and the *Rāmāyaṇa*, that relate interesting stories to illustrate the teachings of Hinduism and the principles of Vedanta.

- *Purāṇas*. Eighteen books, compiled by Vyasa, that dramatize the scriptural truths of the Upanishads in stories about the lives of saints, divine incarnations, and other inspired

[3] For further discussion of the sacred books of India, see Appendix I.

beings. They offer symbolic illustrations of subtle philosophical principles, easily understood by the common man.

The Upanishads still remain the core of India's spiritual heritage. They are the cream of the Vedas. The very word *Upaniṣad* is pregnant with meaning. When you break the word down into its constituent parts, you have:

upa	=	"near"
ni	=	"(approach with) firm determination"
sad	=	"sit"

Thus, as the very word indicates, Vedanta is a knowledge that one should learn near the feet of the master, in an attitude of surrender yet with firm determination. If you read the scriptures as you would an encyclopedia, you will not grasp their true import; Vedantic knowledge will remain an intellectual knowledge only. The student of the Upanishads must, through a process of living, experience firsthand that the Self within him is the supreme Reality everywhere — and thereby break free of the limitations that bind him.

Although the original source of Vedanta is known to be the oral wisdom enshrined in the Upanishads, we can say that Vedanta as we know it today derives from three great textbook categories (*prasthāna traya*):

- The Upanishads. In total, 108 Upanishads have been preserved. Of those, 10 are considered the principal ones: *Aitareya*, *Bṛhadāraṇyaka*, *Chāndogya*, *Īśāvāsya*, *Kaṭha*, *Kena*, *Māṇḍūkya*, *Muṇḍaka*, *Praśna*, and *Taittirīya*.
- The *Bhagavad Gītā*: This eighteen-chapter poem by Vyasa expounds Vedanta in the dynamic setting of a battlefield, where Lord Krishna reveals the teaching of Vedanta to the warrior-prince Arjuna. It constitutes the central portion of

the great epic, the *Mahābhārata*, and contains the cream of the Upanishads.

- The *Brahma Sūtras*. Also known as *Vedānta Sūtras*, this text comprises a series of aphorisms, again attributed to Vyasa, that interpret the Upanishadic teachings.

Mahāvākyas

The quintessence of Vedanta is contained in *mahāvākyas*, great aphoristic declarations of the supreme Truth. They are direct revelations of *Brahman*. The best-known *mahāvākyas* are taken one each from the four Vedas:

- *Prajñānam Brahma* — "Consciousness is *Brahman*." (from *Aitareya Upaniṣad, Ṛg Veda*)
- *Tat tvam asi* — "That thou art." (from *Chāndogya Upaniṣad, Sāma Veda*)
- *Ayam Ātmā Brahma* — "This Self (*Ātman*) is *Brahman*." (from *Māṇḍūkya Upaniṣad, Atharva Veda*)
- *Aham Brahma asmi* — "I am *Brahman*." (from *Bṛhadāraṇyaka Upaniṣad, Yajur Veda*)

Prajñānam Brahma, "Consciousness is *Brahman*," declares that Consciousness, which pulsates in an individual and provides sentience to the matter layers, is the same as the supreme Reality, the substratum of the entire universe. In other words, one and the same Consciousness acts as the common substratum for both the microcosm and the macrocosm.

> Electricity functioning in a small bulb is the same as the electricity that functions in all the electric bulbs, fans, radios, television sets, and countless other pieces of electrical

equipment anywhere in the world. Consciousness is like electricity, one homogeneous power that may have manifold manifestations.

The second *mahāvākya*, *Tat tvam asi*, "That thou art," is probably the best known of the four. It declares: "That infinite, all-pervading Truth is your own essential nature."

tat	=	That	=	The supreme *Brahman*
tvam	=	thou	=	You in your essential nature (the Self)
asi	=	are	=	The two, *Brahman* and *Ātman*, are identical.

The third *mahāvākya* is *Ayam Ātmā Brahma*, "This Self is *Brahman*." *Ayam* means "this" and signifies the self-effulgent Consciousness within. This Consciousness lies deep within the individual, within all the five matter layers, or sheaths. This Self, the innermost core of the personality, is the very same *Brahman* that enlivens the visible universe. This statement may be seen as a practical formula for the seeker to contemplate so as to gradually discover the identity between his Self and the supreme Reality.

The fourth *mahāvākya* is *Aham Brahma asmi*, "I am *Brahman*," which declares that the conscious Principle in ourselves is nothing other than *Brahman*, total Consciousness. *Aham*, meaning "I," refers to the pure Self within, not the limited perceiver-feeler-thinker. This "I" is the same as the all-pervading *Brahman*. The last of the four *mahāvākyas* may be thought of as a statement of the seeker's own experience of self-transcendence and realization of the supreme Self.

For Your Study and Reflection

15. Vedanta

STUDY QUESTIONS, Level 1

1. List the four Vedas by name and describe the fourfold content of each.

2. What is the meaning of the word *Upaniṣad*? What does that meaning tell us about how a seeker of Truth should study?

3. Explain the derivation of the word *Vedānta*.

STUDY QUESTIONS, Level 2

1. Why do you think the oral tradition is a particularly powerful means of transmitting spiritual knowledge?

2. Describe, in detail, the *prasthāna traya*.

3. Explain the meaning of *Tat tvam asi*.

FOR YOUR REFLECTION

- The *Ātman* moves, and It moves not; It is far and It is near; It is within all this, and It is also outside all this. (*Īśāvāsya Upaniṣad* V)

- He who constantly sees everywhere all existence in the Self and the Self in all beings and forms thereafter shrinks not from anything. (*Īśāvāsya Upaniṣad* VI)

- This is *Brahman*, This is Indra, This is creator Prajapati. This is again all the gods and these five great elements, namely, earth, air, space, water, and fire, all the small creatures and the other seeds of creation, the egg-born, the womb-born, the humidity-born, plants and trees, horses, cows, human beings, elephants and all that which is living, the immovable and the flying, and whatever exists — all these are guided and supported by Consciousness. The universe has Consciousness for its guide. Consciousness is the basis for all; verily, Consciousness is *Brahman*. (*Aitareya Upaniṣad* III:I:3)

- All this is verily *Brahman*. This *Ātman* is *Brahman* . . . (*Māṇḍūkya Upaniṣad* 2)

FURTHER READING

- *Aitareya Upaniṣad*. Commentary by Swami Chinmayananda. Bombay, India: Central Chinmaya Mission Trust, 1982. Chapter II, Section I, commentary on verse 3.

Māyā 16

Brahman is pure Consciousness, our real nature. That supreme Reality is omnipresent, omnipotent, and omniscient and the state of absolute knowledge, peace, and bliss. Yet we feel limited, finite, and riddled with pain and sorrow.

How did we "fall" from the heights of our real nature?

Illusion

Vedanta does not accept any real fall from Reality. The Upanishads tirelessly assert that we are none other than the supreme, bliss-filled Reality Itself, as the *mahāvākyas* attest.[1] And yet we feel ignorant, not omniscient; impotent, not omnipotent; agitated, never in a state of sustained peace and bliss. We experience the plurality of the outer world and don't seem to see the oneness affirmed by Vedanta. Yet Vedanta asserts again and again that we are the pure Self and that the world and all its entourage of limitations are but an illusion created by our nonapprehension of our divine nature.

As long as we are alive, we move through three states of consciousness — the waking, the dream, and the deep-sleep sates. In each state, we experience its respective world: the waking world, the dream world, and the deep-sleep world. Vedanta declares that all three worlds are unreal when viewed from the perspective of pure Consciousness. Each of

[1] See Chapter 15, "Vedanta."

the three worlds has a *relative reality* only as long as we remain in the respective state. As we move from one state to the other, the just-abandoned world loses its reality.

> When we glide from the waking state into the dream sate, the reality of the waking world is lost. Similarly, the reality of the dream state vanishes upon waking.

The sages' conclusion was: The waking world has no reason to claim greater reality than that of the dream or the deep-sleep worlds.

The relative reality claimed by the waker with respect to the waking world or by the dreamer with respect to the dream world has been compared to the false superimposition of the impression of a snake on a rope (one of the most famous analogies in Vedantic literature).

> A person walking on a dark forest path sees a curving, thin shape in front of him and steps back in fright: a snake! His heart pounds and his palms sweat. Then another traveler stops by and shines the beam of a flashlight upon the terror-inspiring form on the ground: Instead of a snake, it turns out to be a mere rope!

The rope alone is real. But **nonapprehension** of the rope gives rise to the **misapprehension** of a snake. The snake is an optical illusion; it does not exist in reality. Similarly, *Brahman* alone exists. When *Brahman* is not apprehended (seen), its nonapprehension causes the misapprehension of the phenomenal world. Our entire world and all of our egocentric ideas of separate existence are mere superimpositions upon the one Reality, *Brahman*.

> Nonapprehension of rope → misapprehension of snake → agitation

> Nonapprehension of *Brahman* → misapprehension of phenomenal world → agitation, limitation

Nonapprehension of *Brahman* is called **ignorance** (*avidyā*), the cause for the perception of the pluralistic world. The macrocosmic aspect of *avidyā* — that is, the total ignorance of all beings — is called *māyā*. *Māyā* is therefore said to be the cause for the creation of the world, just as ignorance is the cause for the creation of our subjective world. An individual, Mr. Smith, is "the Self + ignorance"; similarly, *Īśvara*, the Lord of all creation, is "*Brahman* + *māyā*." *Māyā* is described as an inexplicable power inherent in *Brahman*, just as heat is inherent in fire. Fire and heat are inseparable, like the two sides of a coin. So too are *Brahman*, the supreme Reality, and *māyā*, the seed of all creation.

The Play of the *Guṇas*

Māyā manifests itself in the world as three qualities, or *guṇas*.[2] *Brahman* has neither any quality nor any expression of Its own. However, when pure Consciousness is reflected by a "thought pool," It manifests Itself as intelligence or knowledge.

> We can compare *sāttvic* thoughts to the pure, calm surface of a pool of water, *rājasic* thoughts to turbulent water, and *tāmasic* thoughts to dim and dirty water. Just as the sun appears dim in dirty water, so also Consciousness is practically imperceptible in a *tāmasic* mind. In turbulent water, the sun's reflection is bright but unsteady, just as *rājasic* thoughts provide a bright but disturbed reflection of Consciousness. On the calm surface of a quiet pool, the sun's reflection is clear and undisturbed. So also, a *sāttvic* mind is a perfect reflecting medium for Consciousness, which shines through *sāttvic* thoughts clearly and steadily.

When Consciousness functions through a mind that is predominantly *sāttvic*, It expresses Itself as the God-Principle. This Principle manifests Itself as three mighty powers:

---

[2] Recall the discussion in Chapter 12, "Guṇas."

creation, maintenance, and destruction. These three great powers are personified in the divine forms of Brahma, Vishnu, and Shiva, respectively, in order to enable the average person to grasp the idea more easily.

Destruction and creation go hand in hand, as we see everywhere in the world:

> The destruction of the morning is the creation of the evening, and the destruction of the evening is the creation of the night. A tree is maintained by the continuous process of birth and death of the stages of a flower, fruit, seed, seedling, and full-grown tree.

According to the *Purāṇas*, the three deities have the following consorts:

- **Brahma**, God of Creation, is married to Sarasvati, Goddess of Knowledge.
- **Vishnu**, God of Maintenance, is married to Lakshmi, Goddess of Wealth.
- **Shiva**, God of Destruction, is married to Uma, Goddess of Matter. The Divine Mother (who also represents primal energy and power) has many forms, including Parvati and Shakti.

Brahma, in order to create, must possess the knowledge to create; therefore his consort is the Goddess of Knowledge, Sarasvati. Vishnu, who represents the power of maintenance, must have wealth in order to provide for the necessities of life, and therefore he has the Goddess of Wealth, Lakshmi, at his side. Shiva is married to Uma, who represents matter, as the power of destruction can function only in the field of perishable matter.

The chart on page 163 shows the play of the *guṇas* in the world. *Rajas* is the cause of mental agitations in us. These agitations are called *vikṣepa* in Sanskrit. *Tamas* produces an

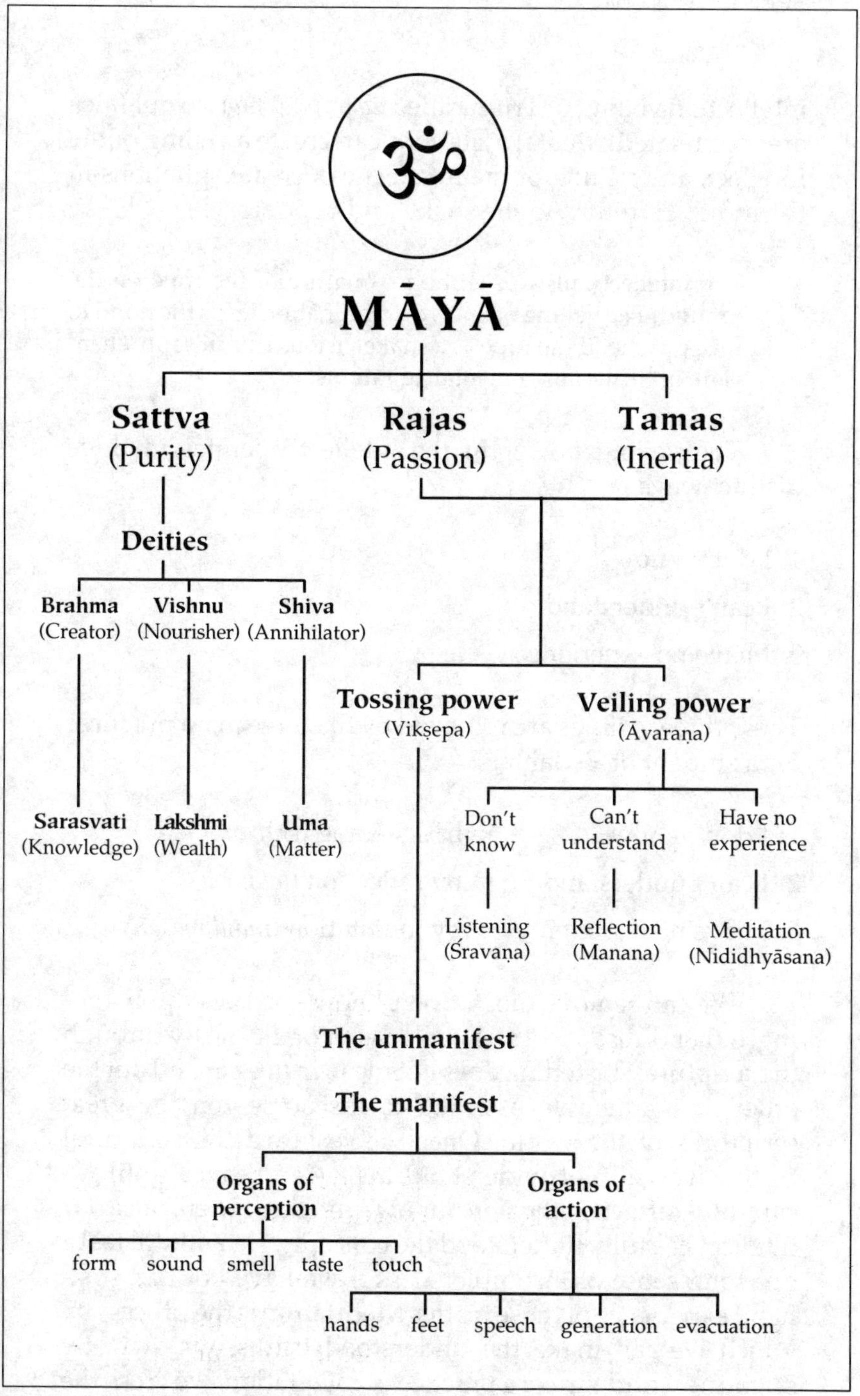
MĀYĀ
Sattva
(Purity)
Rajas
(Passion)
Tamas
(Inertia)
Deities
Brahma
(Creator)
Vishnu
(Nourisher)
Shiva
(Annihilator)
Sarasvati
(Knowledge)
Lakshmi
(Wealth)
Uma
(Matter)
Tossing power
(Vikṣepa)
Veiling power
(Āvaraṇa)
Don't know
Can't understand
Have no experience
Listening
(Śravaṇa)
Reflection
(Manana)
Meditation
(Nididhyāsana)
The unmanifest
The manifest
Organs of perception
Organs of action
form
sound
smell
taste
touch
hands
feet
speech
generation
evacuation

intellectual veiling of Truth called *āvaraṇa*. The two qualities are interrelated: Mental agitations can create a veiling of the intellect, and veiling of the intellect can create agitations in the mind. To return to the snake-and-rope story:

> The intellect fails to see the real nature of the rope on the ground. The veiling of one's discrimination leads the mind to misapprehend the rope as a snake vision. This misapprehension, in turn, causes mental agitations.

The veiling power in the intellect operates in three distinct ways:

1. I don't know.
2. I can't understand.
3. I have no experience.

These three veilings are removed by the three main practices for a student of Vedanta:

1. I don't know → by listening (*śravaṇa*)
2. I can't understand → by reflection (*manana*)
3. I have no experience → by meditation (*nididhyāsana*)

We can remove the "I don't know" obstacle by **listening,** either directly to a spiritual master or indirectly through the scriptures. Listening does not mean in one ear and out the other. It is attentive listening to discourses on the great scriptures of the world. Once we've heard the scriptural truths, we will not understand their significance until we carefully **reflect** on them in our own intellect. Then, once our intellect has fully understood the concepts, we will still feel a gnawing sense of incompleteness if we have not had first-hand experience of those truths. **Meditation** is the process by which we can make the understood truths our own. By sustained and sincere practice of meditation, we cross the last phase of the veiling power and experience union with pure Consciousness, which supports not only us but the entire universe.

Frequently people tell me that they have gone through the *Gītā* many times. I tell them: "Let the *Gītā* go through *you* — at least once! It will do you more good." Not just hearing or reading, but absorbing the great ideas contained in the scriptures, assimilating them, and living the values expressed therein will produce a radiance in our lives.

Besides producing the veiling power, the *rajas-tamas* quality also produces agitations in the mind. Agitations manifest themselves in the world as perceptions and actions through the ten organs of perception and action. With such manifestation through the physical body, the seeming "fall" has taken place — from the heights of the transcendental glory of the supreme Reality to a finite, limited mortal.

But we know that Vedanta declares: You are that — you are that infinite, blissful Self. To regain that blissful nature which is always yours, but veiled by the three *guṇas*, you have to reduce the *rajas-tamas* impurity, thus increasing the *sāttvic* component of your nature. When you develop *sattva* to its absolute purity, you are poised to transcend the *guṇas*, to move beyond even the smallest trace of *sattva* into the state of Self-realization.

Thus, realizing the pure Self as your own is not a matter of gaining a new stature from some external source. You only need to remove the ignorance that covers your innately pure and blissful nature. To remove that layer of ignorance, you need to engage in the three main *sādhanās* (practices) of Vedanta: listening, reflection, and meditation.[3]

Relationship to *Om*

Depending on our particular mix of *guṇas*, we see the world — as well as our relationship to the supreme Reality — differently.

To an ordinary person, his body is himself. His

[3] Chapter 18, "Sādhanā," will cover spiritual practices in greater depth.

identification with the body is deep and strong. He lives for the body, strives for the body, and knows no other mission in life than seeking sensuous enjoyments. For one who exists in such a state, the only relationship to the supreme Reality can be one of **separateness**.

To another class of people — who have evolved to recognize that they are not only their bodies but are also beings endowed with a mind and intellect — to such people, the human being is not just a perishable worm, but a sacred creature who possesses almost godly powers evident in the manifestations of the mind and intellect. Such people study the achievements of science and poetry. They recognize the great thinkers and discoverers. They take into account the victory that man has so far gained over mighty Nature. They see man as a thinking creature who has a glory and might not much inferior to God's. For people with this degree of development, the relationship with Reality is that of being **a part of the whole.**

For these two categories of humanity, India has provided two approaches to Truth:

- **Dualism** (*Dvaita*; main exponent — Sri Madhvacharya) concludes that the Lord and His devotee will ever remain as two distinct entities. The relationship of the devotee to the Lord is one of complete surrender in love and reverence. The supreme goal of humankind is to reach His feet and remain there eternally, ever in His service.

- **Qualified Nondualism or Monism** (*Viśiṣṭādvaita*; main exponent — Sri Ramanuja) contends that the devotee is part of the whole, the Lord, not separate from Him.

The third approach, that of Advaita Vedanta, unequivocally declares a yet different relationship:

- **Nondualism or Monism** (*Advaita Vedānta*; main exponent — Sri Shankaracharya) says: Man is in essence God.

To a student of Dualism or Qualified Monism, this declaration of Vedanta may appear fantastic, for the former views Truth in reference to his body while the latter views It with reference to his psychological personality. The perfect student of Vedanta, however, discovers through discrimination that neither his body nor his mind-intellect equipment is really himself. He feels that some power subtler than the mind and intellect plays hide-and-seek within him and forms a dynamic life center deep within the matter envelopments. The guru endorses the disciple's conclusions, provides him with arguments and convictions, and leads him to the seat of life, the Self, that lies within the seeker himself. When the disciple comes to understand the significance of the guru's words and experiences, firsthand, that he himself is That which he has been seeking, he gains perfect knowledge. He is Self-realized.

In the *Rāmāyaṇa*, we find the three kinds of relationship to Truth beautifully described by Hanuman, the greatest devotee of Sri Rama, as he relates his relationship to his guru:

> Hanuman says, "O Lord, at moments when I am steeped in my body consciousness, I am Your slave. When I identify myself with my mind and intellect, I am a part of You. And when I am one with my own nature, as the spirit, I am Yourself."

Our relationship with Reality can thus be explained in three different ways, depending on our state of mind. Even the greatest sage has moments when he is conscious of the sorrows of physical pain and the inclemencies of weather. At such moments, even he may fall prostrate at the Lord's feet and mentally seek His mercy. At other moments, he may be conscious of some inner mental agitation or irresistible poetic outburst and may recognize within himself a power that is almost a part of the Lord Himself. And then, in those rare moments when he has completely retired from the outer coverings of matter to the subtlest of the subtle within, he sees that "I am That." At that point the individual and the supreme Reality constitute one perfect whole.

These three schools of thought are not so much competing and contradicting theories, as explanations of necessary stages we must pass through in our pilgrimage to the peak of perfection. Only the intellectual pundits quarrel and seek to establish one or the other declaration as superior. The moment we step on the path of spiritual practice, we'll realize that these three are three wayside inns for our pilgrimage. We can rest at each and proceed ahead. Every pilgrim must first visit Madhvacharya, from where he proceeds to worship Ramanuja; then alone can he reach the portals of Vedanta, the abode of Sri Shankaracharya, where he can find his ultimate release from the thralldom of *māyā*.

For Your Study and Reflection

16. Māyā

STUDY QUESTIONS, Level 1

1. Explain the nature of *Brahman* and of *māyā* by using the snake-rope example.

2. Explain how the three powers that Brahma, Vishnu, and Shiva represent are necessary for the existence of the phenomenal world.

3. Explain how the spiritual practices of *listening, reflection,* and *meditation* work together in promoting progress on the spiritual path.

STUDY QUESTIONS, Level 2

1. Can you think of any events from your life where one event was seen very differently — was perceived as a very different reality — by each of several observers? How does such an occurrence relate to *māyā*?

2. Explain why *māyā* is considered the cause for the creation of the world.

3. From what you know about two of the major religions of the world (for instance, Judaism and Islam), how would you describe their main approach to Truth — as that of Dualism, Qualified Monism, or Advaita Vedanta?

FOR YOUR REFLECTION

- In the dream state, even though there is no contact with the outside world, the mind alone projects the entire dream universe of the enjoyer. Similarly, the waking state is no different. All this [world of pluralistic phenomena] is but a projection of the mind. (Shankaracharya, *Vivekacūḍāmaṇi* 170)

- It [*māyā*] is neither existent nor nonexistent, nor both; neither same nor different, nor both; neither made up of parts nor whole, nor both. Most wonderful it is and beyond description in words. (Shankaracharya, *Vivekacūḍāmaṇi* 109)

- Nescience (*avidyā*), or *māyā*, is also called the unmanifest, and is the power of the Lord. It is without beginning; it comprises the three *guṇas* and is superior to their effects. From the effects it produces, it is to be inferred only by one who has a clear intellect. It is this *avidyā* which projects the entire universe. (Shankaracharya, *Vivekacūḍāmaṇi* 108)

- By realization of the pure, nondual *Brahman*, *māyā* can be destroyed, just as the illusion of the snake is removed by the discriminative knowledge of the rope. Its *guṇas* are *rajas*, *tamas*, and *sattva*, distinguished by their respective functions. (Shankaracharya, *Vivekacūḍāmaṇi* 110)

- Everything is due to the effect of *māyā* — from Mahat down to the gross body. Know thou that these and *māyā* itself are the not-Self; therefore, they are unreal, like the mirage waters in the desert. (Shankaracharya, *Vivekacūḍāmaṇi* 123)

FURTHER READING

Shankaracharya, *Vivekachoodamani* (*Vivekacūḍāmaṇi*). Commentary by Swami Chinmayananda. Bombay: Central Chinmaya Mission Trust, 1987. Verses 120-144.

Self-Realization 17

Breaking through the matter layers to discover the ultimate Reality at the core of our being is our sole and sacred vocation as spiritual students. The consummation of that great effort is Self-realization, or liberation (*mokṣa*).

The Upanishads give many indications about the realized person, but the references lie scattered in the pages of those sacred texts. The signs of a Self-realized person were first compiled in the *Bhagavad Gītā* by Veda Vyasa in the concluding eighteen verses of Chapter II. In those verses we see a portrait of an individual who is liberated even while living (*jīvanmukta*). Similarly, the great Vedantin, Sri Shankaracharya, adopted a similar technique in painting a picture of a person of perfection in *Vivekacūḍāmaṇi*.

Steady Wisdom

The Self-realized person is a dynamic person of action. In order to understand him, we must understand him as he lives in the world, not as he sits under a tree lost in contemplation. We must peep into the world through his mind:

- How does he see the world?
- How does he react to problems?
- How does he relate himself to others?

A realized person is a dynamic, pulsating individual whose every moment of existence is dedicated to the service of humankind. He need not be retired from the community. We can view him right in the marketplace — downtown, in the midst of the calamitous, competitive world of temptations. A person who keeps his composure and who remains ever rooted in pure Consciousness in the midst of such turbulence is called one of steady wisdom (*sthitaprajña*).

A person of steady wisdom functions in the world with total freedom. Physically he demands nothing; emotionally he has no encumbrances; intellectually he is extremely brilliant at all times because he has no hang-ups whatever. Such a person, functioning freely in the world as a master of all situations as well as of his own physical, mental, and intellectual equipment, is so contrary to all our expectations and experiences that an average student of Vedanta will not be able to appreciate him unless the teacher paints at least a vague picture of him. Only then will the student see the full beauty of the one who is totally uninhibited; completely free; joyously living in the world; actively participating in the history-making processes around him; serving everyone, while exhibiting infinite love, mercy, kindness, and forgiveness at all times; and uncompromisingly living his perfection in the midst of all worldly things.

In *Vivekacūḍāmaṇi*, Shankaracharya paints a vivid picture of such a person. In the portrait that emerges from verse to verse, we see the emotional, physical, and intellectual attitudes of a person of perfection toward the world of things and beings:

> *No thought for the enjoyments of the past, no thought for the future, and indifference even to the present — this is an indication of a liberated person* (jīvanmukta)*. (Vivekacūḍāmaṇi* 433*)*

A liberated person is one who neither cares to remember the past nor wants to waste time worrying about the future. She refuses to draw the past into the present by way of memory. As for the future, why worry about it? It will look after itself.

We are generally anxious about the present because we think that our happiness depends upon the present situation: We think we can gain our physical, mental, and intellectual satisfaction from various things and their arrangements. The master who is revelling in the Truth is indifferent even to the present. Objects and situations may be available or may not be—so what? If they are, fine; if they are not, never mind. The master's source of joy, an inexhaustible storehouse of bliss and beatitude, is within himself. Thus, he can be totally unconcerned about the present.

The world is by its very nature pluralistic, consisting of different qualities of goodness and evil. In this world, the good and the bad, the vicious and the noble, the wicked and the good are all mixed together. However, in this seeming plurality the liberated one sees only the manifestation of the one divine Reality. The one who has realized one's Self has realized the same Self everywhere. "I" in one particular form is a rascal, and "I" in another form is divine. The divinity and the rascality are only qualities and textures of the mind. Behind the mind is the one infinite Self.

> Depending on the color of the bulb through which light manifests itself, the light may appear to be different colors, but that which is manifesting itself in these various ways is but one electricity.

Wickedness in any person is the result of the "curvature" of his mind and intellect, of the false values that he is living. However, even for living those false values, Life is necessary. Life is one. The Self is one. But each individual possesses his own particular quality while manifesting himself in the world, which is a mixture of good, bad, and indifferent. When I look at the world from the level of my body, mind, and intellect, I give it the validity of that level and start running away from the wicked and toward the good. All the distinctions I experience—"I hate these people" or "I love those people," that is, all likes and dislikes (*rāga* and *dveṣa*) — are natural at this level.

The perfected being is one who recognizes all these distinctions as the expressions of the one divine Reality alone. He sees the Lord in and through everything, here through wickedness, there through meritorious works, but he always sees that same One only. Such a sage knows neither hatred for a thing nor great fascinating attachment to something else.

While good and bad situations are kaleidoscopically changing all around him at all times, the perfected being, because of his experience of the Self, sees all with equal vision. He who has discovered the source of all happiness can afford the luxury of watching the play of the world around him, just as the person watching a tragedy in a movie theater may weep while witnessing it, yet at the same time enjoy it.

The Self-realized person is one who has equal vision toward everything around him. You and I usually dance in joy when good situations arise, and we sit and cry when bad situations come to plague us. The liberated one neither cries not dances. He is equanimous.

Inner and Outer

For one who is enjoying the bliss of the higher state of Consciousness, all thoughts of the mind and intellect are ever engaged in experiencing that bliss. The liberated individual does not know what is within and what is without; for these "within" and "without" are with reference to the body only. That which is behind or within the body is called the "inner life" or the "inner world." The "outside world" is outside the body. The body is the frontier with reference to which we say "within" or "inner" and "without" or "outer," just as we say the lecture is inside the hall — inside the four walls of the lecture hall. The next lecture is outside, outside the four walls of the hall.

A liberated person is one who no longer recognizes the

reality of the body. When no body reference exists, where is "within" or "without"?

> The dreamer, while dreaming, experiences an outer world and an inner world. Let us say that he is afraid of situations developing in the outer world of his dream, situations about which he is unhappy. When the dreamer awakens to become the waker, from the waker's standpoint the inner and outer world of the dreamer no longer exist. The inner and the outer have merged.

So long as we are living as individual egos, identified with our bodies, it is natural for us to talk of the "inner self" or the "inner reality" and of the "outer world" of situations. When the ego has merged in the Self, from the standpoint of the realized person, there is no longer an "inner" or "outer," because body perception has dissolved. In deep sleep, we experience utter darkness, nonapprehension, ignorance. That darkness of deep sleep—is it inside us or outside us? Because in deep sleep we are not conscious of the body, we can talk of neither "inside" nor "outside."

Thus, once a person has reached the state of higher Consciousness, he does not understand anything of "inside" or "outside." The experience is one of all-pervading Consciousness alone — like the sky or like space, ever present everywhere.

A master also has no more misconceptions such as "I am the body" or "These sense organs are mine." In regard to the duties pertaining to the body, no ideas of possession arise. Security, shelter, possessions, comforts, food, breathing, talking, seeing, hearing, smelling, touching—all these are duties (*dharmas*) pertaining to the body and the sense organs. Thus we may say, "I want to hear that; I would like to see that," all the time using "I" to mean the body. The perfected person remains indifferent to all *dharmas* of the body. It never occurs to him to think, "I must see" or "I must hear" or "I must eke out at least a little bit of joy from the world outside." Already satiated with the infinite bliss that he is experiencing, he has become indifferent to the body and the sense organs and their *dharmas*. Whatever is, is all right.

As Shankaracharya says:

> *He who has no ego with regard to the body, the sense organs, and so on, nor has the concept of "this" with regard to other things, he is considered a liberated person. (Vivekacūḍāmaṇi* 439)

Just as on waking up from the dream we are released from all the sorrows and imperfections of the dreamer, one who is Self-realized has awakened to the Reality and is liberated from the sorrowful bondages of plurality. The "I-ness" of the body and the sense organs and the perception of all other things as "this, this, this" — objects separate from oneself — are distinctions that never occur to a person of perfection. Generally, we see only plurality through the sense organs. When we cease to identify with the body and the sense organs, everything merges into the One.

The liberated person's realization is:

- The changeless Essence in me (*Ātman*) and the substratum of the whole universe (*Brahman*) are one and the same.
- The Self in me is the Self everywhere.
- The substratum of the whole universe, *Brahman*, is playing as the pluralistic phenomenal world.

This realization is similar to what we experience on waking up from a dream:

> The waker realizes that the dreamer and the dream objects were all essentially one: that there is no distinction between "I-dreamer" and "I-waker"; that the waker "I" is the same as the dreamer "I"; and that the dream universe — the dream

sun, moon, and stars — all arose from the one mind only.

Just as on waking from the dream we realize that between the dreamer, the dream, and the waker there is no distinction at all, so also a liberated person realizes that the Self in him is the Self everywhere, the same Self that used to play about as names and forms in the phenomenal world that he once experienced as an ego. An individual who has realized that the individual ego (*jīva*), the universe (*jagat*), and the Lord (*Īśvara*) are all merged into one is a *jīvanmukta*, one liberated even while living.

Perfect Balance

Whether the body is beaten by the wicked or revered by the good, the one who is mentally quiet and balanced is unaffected. We are not like that. Whenever we are adored or respected or revered a little, we float beyond the clouds in joy. Our adorers may at that point tell us that they have now found more worthy objects of adoration. Boom! — we come down. We are always like that: We go up and then come down again. In the case of a person of steady wisdom, even when fools and the wicked cannot understand what he is doing and literally beat him down, he still remains a fountain of love, compassion, understanding, and forgiveness. He is never disturbed; he remains ever the same, in balance and equipoise.

We tend to lose our balance because we identify with the body-mind-intellect, which have no stability. The three are ever changing and therefore are constantly pulling us up and down. Because the perfected being has ended all identifications and has awakened to the steady and changeless Essence, he retains his balance even when he is expressing himself through the body-mind-intellect equipment. Even though the body and mind go through various experiences, he is never affected by them because he is not *in* the equipment; the equipment is in *him*.

Even though sense objects are available to her, the

person of perfection has no more desire or need for them, because she has already found infinite happiness. Objects of pleasure may be brought to her by devotees and others. Even then, they reach her only as rivers reach the ocean. But she is never flooded, she never gets excited to overflowing; she has no desire to hug the sense objects even though they come to her. She is permanently peaceful and serene and sufficient unto herself.

> The vast network of rivers streams into the ocean, yet the flow of the myriad rivers makes no difference to the ocean. Similarly, objects may come to the one who is liberated while living and yet nothing happens. He is ever merged in pure Consciousness.

In all liberated souls the common factor is peace, tranquillity. Those liberated from the thralldom of the body, mind, and intellect are not disturbed by any circumstance whatsoever. They abide ever in the Self — serene, fulfilled, and ever ready to give of their fullness and love to others.

For Your Study and Reflection

17. Self-Realization

STUDY QUESTIONS, Level 1

1. Name three characteristics of the realized person and explain them.

2. What is meant by the sentence "Wickedness in any person is the result of the 'curvature' of his mind and intellect"?

3. In the dream analogy, who is parallel to the realized being? Why?

STUDY QUESTIONS, Level 2

1. Explain how a liberated person doesn't perceive things in terms of "inner" and "outer."

2. Explain how the following stanza describes a Self-realized person:

   That which is night to all beings, in that the self-controlled man wakes; where all beings are awake, that is the night for the sage who sees. (*Bhagavad Gītā* II:69)

3. If the realized person sees all beings as manifestations of the ever-pure *Brahman*, do you think he can distinguish between "good" and "bad" people? Explain your answer.

FOR YOUR REFLECTION

- When a man completely casts off, O Partha, all the desires of the mind and is satisfied in the Self by the Self, then is he said to be one of steady wisdom. (*Bhagavad Gītā* II:55)

- The sort of mental activity which admits only the identity of the Self and *Brahman*, free from all limitations and devoid of duality, concerned only with pure Knowledge, is called illumination. One who has this steady illumination is known as a person of steady wisdom. (Shankaracharya, *Vivekacūḍāmaṇi* 428)

- When confronted with things pleasing or painful, to be unperturbed in both cases, maintaining an equal attitude — this is an indication of a *jīvanmukta*. (Shankaracharya, *Vivekacūḍāmaṇi* 435)

FURTHER READING

- *The Holy Geeta* (*Bhagavad Gītā*). Commentary by Swami Chinmayananda. Bombay: Central Chinmaya Mission Trust, 1980. Chapter II, verses 54-71.

- Shankaracharya, *Vivekachoodamani* (*Vivekacūḍāmaṇi*). Commentary by Swami Chinmayananda. Bombay: Central Chinmaya Mission Trust, 1987. Verses 426-445.

Sādhanā 18

To reach the pinnacle of peace, fulfillment, and tranquillity called Self-realization, we have to work on cleaning away from our real nature the accumulated conditionings that hide its pristine beauty. That process of cleansing is called *spiritual practice*, or *sādhanā* in Sanskrit.

Progress on the Path

The material world generally accepts quantitative evaluations as measures of prosperity and success:

- How much have you earned?
- How much did you save, produce, sell, and acquire?

Material success depends on how much, how many, or how often. Spiritual seekers habitually apply the same quantitative measures in estimating their own inner achievements. Automatically they congratulate themselves on the quantity of their "glorious *sādhanā*." However, quantitative measures are false indicators of spiritual progress.

In spiritual practice, it is not how much we read, but how much we understand and reflect and meditate upon the concepts that assures success. The quality, intensity, sincerity, devotion, understanding, and enthusiasm of the heart with which we do our *sādhanā* determine the true heights to which we rise in our self-mastery.

Spiritual seekers often suffer chronically from lack of progress on the path. From their diaries, it is clear that if quantity alone were demanded in spiritual practice, such seekers would have nothing more to do. And yet their experience is that they find themselves exactly where they were three years ago. Indeed, it is a painful disappointment. The cure for such seekers is easy to prescribe, but perhaps more difficult to practice. What they need is a sharpened tempo in their spiritual seeking: a quickening of perception, an alertness of the soul, and a warmer ardency in their embrace of the goal. These qualities cannot be developed by themselves, one at a time; but seekers will find themselves absorbing them when their minds gain a deeper harmony.

Harmony comes as a result of two processes:

1. Discrimination (*viveka*): The positive process of gaining a clear picture of the all-satisfying goal and the straight path to it.
2. Detachment, dispassion (*vairāgya*): The negative process of detaching from all dissipating urges.

Once these two qualities are carefully cultivated and fully developed — discriminating appreciation of the Real and detachment from the false — the rest of the pilgrimage becomes pleasant and sure, though in no way easy.

Discrimination (*Viveka*)

A mind that rushes out into the world of objects is full of desires and agitations. Such a state of mind is not conducive to quiet contemplation upon the Truth. Withdrawal of the mind from preoccupation with the world quiets the agitations in it and prepares the ground for contemplation. In such a calmed mental atmosphere, the intellect begins to distinguish between the ephemeral objects of the world and the eternal Principle of life. In other words, we learn to discriminate between:

- The Real and the unreal
- The Changeless and the changing
- The Imperishable and the perishable

We all have experience with discrimination in our daily lives:

> We discriminate between good coffee and bad. We can distinguish a loyal friend from a fickle one. We know how to be very discriminating in choosing our next car, house, or stereo set.

Now let's try to apply discrimination to the spiritual field:

> We know that time is a product of the mind; it has no separate existence from the mind. We also know that *Brahman*, the supreme Reality, transcends the mind; therefore, *Brahman* cannot be bound by time. Even though we may not yet experience the nature of *Brahman* directly, we can have the intellectual conviction of Its timeless, unchangeable nature. Once that conviction becomes strong in us, we inherit the consequent ability to reject all that which is impermanent.

In this way, we learn to discriminate between the Permanent and the impermanent, the Changeless and the changing, the unconditional Self and our various conditionings. As Shankaracharya says:

> *By a process of negation of the conditionings* (upādhis) *through the help of the scriptural statement "Not this, not this"* (neti, neti), *the oneness of the individual soul and the supreme Soul, as indicated by the great* mahāvākyas, *is realized*. (Shankaracharya, *Ātma Bodha* 30)

We, as seekers of Truth, analyze our various conditionings (*upādhis*) — the body and the sense objects it perceives, the mind and its feelings, the intellect and its thoughts. With our power of discrimination, we reject every one of them as the not-Self. We reject even time, space, and causality as perceptions of the mind and intellect. In this process of negation (*neti, neti* — "Not this, not this"), we realize that we are none of these not-Self vestures, but the pure, supreme Self Itself.

Detachment (*Vairāgya*)

Once the mind knows discrimination between the Real and the unreal, detachment follows of its own. Even our daily experiences prove that detachment flows naturally from understanding:

> In your dream, you get married to a lovely person, and you love her dearly. Once you awaken, you cannot maintain your attachment to that dream-love, for the moment you're awake you realize the falsehood of the dream, so your mind quite effortlessly rolls away from your dream attachment.

Before our minds can be fit for higher contemplation and finally for the realization of the divine Self, we have to develop our sense of detachment from the fascinations of the world, and we have to cultivate such detachment *at the mental level*. We cannot achieve true detachment by mere physical retirement from the world, but rather, by maintaining a proper mental relationship to it. We have to renounce our infatuation with the extroverted life and explore the possibility of rediscovering the pure Self deep within.

The word *detachment* has often been misunderstood. For many it holds an uncanny fear, for it seems to point more to a condition of living death than to a state of a better and fuller life. Others have found it as an excuse to escape their obligatory duties and to abandon life overall. Every human being has a purpose in life and should use the world to fulfill it. In fact, the Hindu way of life prescribes that we live a life of *dharma,* that is, that we fulfill the duties that our nature imposes on us.[1] The world provides a field for exhausting our inherent tendencies, our *vāsanās.* But while on the path of evolution we often fall prey to the bewitching objects of the world and our infatuation with our loved ones. These worldly attractions distract us from our goal. The advice of the scriptures is: While remaining in the world, learn to maintain the right relationship to it. We can practice detachment from the world by questioning ourselves thus:

- Who is my wife? husband? mother? father?
- Who was my father before I was born? Who was my husband before I married him? How have I developed an attachment to him?
- Where was my daughter before I gave birth to her?
- Where was I before I appeared in this world?

By reflecting on these questions over and over again, we develop detachment from the usual fascinations of the external world. In time, we will come to the final question:

- Who am I?

Once we start asking such self-introspecting questions, we kindle in ourselves the desire to seek the pure Self, which lies beyond all bonds we may feel with objects and beyond any attachments we may cherish to other human beings.

Even as we release ourselves from the false relationships to the world, we must establish ourselves in the Higher aspects of life. We need to *substitute attachment to the Higher for detachment from the lower.* For this purpose, the scriptures

[1] For a more detailed discussion of *dharma,* see Appendix I.

advise us to cultivate healthy contacts at all levels of the personality by:

- Associating with good people
- Maintaining noble emotions
- Studying and reflecting upon the scriptural truths

Maintenance of such contacts with the higher values of life is called *satsang* (*satsaṅga* in Sanskrit, "good company"). Satsang helps us to stabilize our sense of detachment, and with detachment disappears our deluded vision of the world. We can think of satsang as a fortress we build around ourselves to protect us against the temptations that we encounter in our daily lives. Many things, events, and people will try to pull us away from the spiritual path. The chances are good that despite our knowledge and determination to stay on the path, we will be lured away from it through the influence of people with lower goals. Therefore, for the spiritual seeker, to seek out the "company of the good" is of paramount importance. As a result of the influence of satsang, the mind develops the capacity to withdraw from the usual fields of attraction in the world and to find the calm atmosphere of dispassion.

Another source of extreme attachment is the physical body, for we all share a common weakness to pamper it. The body has no doubt its part to play both in material and spiritual progress, but to spend an entire lifetime in merely beautifying it and meeting its endless demands is, besides being quite out of proportion to the returns gained, detrimental to our progress. The body assumes a special glory as long as life exists, but as soon as the breath leaves it, those near and dear to us are even repelled by its sight. This shows that the respect the body does enjoy during its life is not because of the physical structure itself; any glory it has is lent to it by the Life Principle pulsating in it.

Spiritual students must develop a new relationship to the body and its worldly enjoyments. The right attitude would be to play about in the world as in a field of sport and to consider secular activities as hobbies — all the while maintaining a constant vision of the ultimate goal of human existence, that is, realization of one's true Self. However, many of us allow ourselves to be entangled with life's activities, ever postponing our deeper spiritual practice:

- In childhood, we waste our days in play. Our fascination is with toys and games.
- In youth, we consume our time with pursuits of lust and passion. Although our attachment to toys has fallen away, we waste our time and energy by courting the objects of our love.
- In the middle years of our life, we are busy aggrandizing for ourselves and our family material goods labeled "mine" and "ours."
- In old age, our mind is riddled with agitations, being constantly worried over one thing or another.

Thus, at every stage of our lives, we are constantly preoccupied with one demand or another, finding neither the time nor the inclination to turn toward the Divine. In life, we cannot expect to be completely free of worldly entanglements; to wait for such a time before we undertake the spiritual path is absurd. It is like waiting for the waves to subside in the ocean before taking a swim in the sea!

Therefore, if we as spiritual students are to make any progress on our path, we have to cultivate mental dispassion for the enchantments of the particular stage of life in which we find ourselves.

Six Qualities

In *Vivekacūḍāmaṇi*, Shankaracharya outlines four qualifications of the fit student of Vedanta:

1. discrimination (*viveka*)
2. detachment (*vairāgya*)
3. six mental qualities (*śama*, etc.)
4. burning desire for liberation (*mumukṣutva*)

The four qualities are those determining factors in a seeker that can ensure success. The degree to which the four are present in a seeker, to that degree his success in spiritual endeavors is assured. The first two, discrimination and detachment, we have already discussed. Next are the six mental qualities that help the seeker gain control of the mind:

1. calmness (*śama*)
2. self-control (*dama*)
3. self-withdrawal (*uparati*)
4. forbearance (*titikṣa*)
5. faith (*śraddhā*)
6. tranquillity (*samādhāna*)

Calmness (*śama*) is a condition experienced by the mind when it does not function in worldly activities, but is quietly contemplating the supreme goal. On the other hand, **self-control** (*dama*) is a discipline concerned with the outer field of activity, the discipline of controlling the sense organs. To withdraw the mental rays that shoot out through the sense organs for the perception of their respective objects of pleasure and to absorb those rays within the sense organs is self-control. When one has gained a degree of proficiency in calmness and self-control, **self-withdrawal** (*uparati*) automatically takes place. In self-withdrawal, the seeker's mental condition is such that it is no longer affected by disturbances created by external objects.

When we first learn of these requirements of a spiritual student, we may find them very delicate, difficult, and distressing feats, but in fact the more we practice them, the more we understand that these qualities describe the state of mind of anyone who is trying to execute any great work. Even on the material plane, we find that these qualifications are essential for a person who wants success in his activities. In successful business people, we can observe a certain amount of self-control within and without, as well as self-withdrawal, at least while they are at the desk. However, the spiritual seeker needs a subtlety a million times greater than the materialist.

The fourth psychological qualification indicating spiritual stamina is **forbearance** or **silent endurance** (*titikṣa*). Meek surrender and silent suffering are glorified in all the religions of the world. Even to bring about a revolution in the outer world, the revolutionaries are called upon to make silent sacrifices. How much more essential, then, is forbearance for the inner revolution of an individual who is trying to free himself from his psychological and intellectual confinement! This capacity of the mind to accommodate cheerfully all vicissitudes of life and patiently ignore any obstacles is *titikṣa*.

Unfortunately, many people indulge in acts of perversion in the name of *titikṣa*. They persecute themselves physically and mentally in the name of spiritual seeking, and as a result of their self-persecution, all they gain at the end is a crooked, ugly, deformed mind. Discarding one's clothes or starving oneself to a skinny existence, denying the body its bare necessities or giving unnecessary pain to the mind, running away from life or preserving oneself on an inhuman diet in solitary caves, living an animal's life exposed to a brutal climate or breaking the body in an effort to make it endure more discomforts — none of these is true *titikṣa*. True forbearance is the result of the mind being governed by an intellectual conviction that the divine goal of life is fulfillment through Self-realization; when that conviction is firm, the mind cooperates and faces all difficulties and obstacles to reach the goal. Such a firm person alone is fit for realizing the pure Self.

Since every situation, of its own nature, must keep on changing, it would be foolish to get upset at every change. It is wisdom to suffer adversities meekly, with the comfort and consolation of the knowledge of their finite nature. It is the attitude of the wise to go through life, in joy and in sorrow, in success and in failure, with the constant awareness: "Even this will pass away."

Strong **faith** (*śraddhā*) in one's ideal is the fifth qualification of a spiritual aspirant. *Śraddhā* is not blind faith, as it is often misunderstood by those who have not carefully analyzed it. Shankara is very clear in his definition of *śraddhā* as a healthy attempt to gain a clear intellectual appreciation of the secret significance underlying the words of the scriptures and the teacher. The scriptures give us, through the technique of suggestion, as clear a description of the infinite Truth as is possible through finite sounds and words. Being beyond the mind, pure Consciousness cannot be defined by words; therefore, the supreme goal of human evolution can only be *indicated* by the scriptures. An honest and sincere effort on the part of the student is absolutely necessary if the words indicating the Truth are to be correctly interpreted, understood, and made use of. This capacity to realize the words of the scriptures in all their suggestiveness is called *śraddhā*.

The last of the six great qualifications is **tranquillity** (*samādhāna*). In Shankara's definition, *samādhāna* is a state of poise and tranquillity that the mind gains when it is trained to revel continuously in the concept of a perfect ideal.

> When we are on the ground, our neighbors may be a nuisance to us. We may even argue over the boundaries of our property. But when we take off in a plane, these bickerings seem to have no meaning. From those heights, "my property" and "my neighbor's property" seem to merge into one unbroken

expanse. In an aerial view of the world, there are no mental agitations, because in that vision of oneness, the differences of opinion about boundary lines pale into significance.

Similarly, when a spiritual aspirant raises himself into the greater ambits of spiritual vision, his mind can no longer entertain any agitations at the ordinary level of likes and dislikes. This inner poise, gained as a result of constant contemplation of the supreme Reality, is called *samādhāna*.

These six qualifications are essential in the psychological makeup of a fully evolved seeker, who alone can walk the last lap of the journey with success.

Burning Desire for Liberation

The six qualifications cannot bear fruit unless they grow in a heart watered by discrimination and detachment and ploughed with an intense **desire for liberation** (*mumukṣutva*). When an individual develops his subtle discrimination enough to recognize the depth of life's weaknesses, he develops a pressing urgency for liberation.

A seeker once asked his guru about the meaning of *mumukṣutva*. Without a word, the master took the student by the hand and led him to the nearby river. There, he grabbed the student by the neck and pushed his head into the water, holding it immersed for many long seconds. When he finally released his hold and the student grabbed frantically for some gulps of air, the teacher said, "When you want to realize God as much as you just yearned to get a breath of air, you will have a burning desire for liberation."

Mumukṣutva is not an idle enthusiasm to gain an unknown goal through some mysterious intervention of a god or a teacher. The seeker must be clear about the goal and the various techniques and paths by which he can attain it. The inner revolution of turning the mind's attention away from the external world to discover the divine depths of one's inner nature cannot be accomplished as a half-hearted hobby.

It can only be the result of a lifelong dedication and a full-time endeavor. A seeker who is ready to live every moment of his life in diligent pursuit of the Real is a *mumukṣu,* one consumed by a burning desire for liberation.

In the final analysis, Self-unfoldment must come to express itself in your own heart. As long as it is loaded down with base urges, motives, and schemes, the self-shackled heart cannot "take off" from its fields of sorrow and restlessness into the cloudless sky of spiritual freedom. Break those shackles by cultivating the four qualities of a sincere spiritual seeker and make the mind-intellect vehicle light enough for take-off into the heights of meditative bliss.

For Your Study and Reflection

18. Sādhanā

STUDY QUESTIONS, Level 1

1. In preparing your mind for meditation, what do you think needs to come first, detachment (*vairāgya*) or discrimination (*viveka*)? Why?

2. After we rise beyond our fascination for the body, what do you think is the next attachment to overcome? Give examples to illustrate your point.

3. Give examples from daily life of how application of self-control, self-withdrawal, or forbearance bring about a more sure guarantee of success.

STUDY QUESTIONS, Level 2

1. Analyze the following verse:

   When youthfulness has passed, where is lust and its play? When water has evaporated, where is the lake? When wealth is reduced, where is the retinue? When the Truth is realized, where is saṁsāra *(the world of ceaseless change)?* (Shankaracharya, *Bhaja Govindam* 10)

   What process of the mind (discrimination or dispassion) is illustrated in this verse?

2. Describe the difference between forbearance (*titikṣa*) and the meek submissiveness of a person with a weak mind.

3. Explain how discrimination (*viveka*) enhances the desire for liberation (*mumukṣutva*).

FOR YOUR REFLECTION

- A firm conviction in the intellect that *Brahman* alone is real and the phenomenal world is unreal is known as discrimination between the Real and the unreal. (Shankaracharya, *Vivekacūḍāmaṇi* 20)

- The desire to give up all transitory enjoyments gained through seeing, hearing, and so on, and also experiences gained through the equipment, ranging from a mortal body to the form of Brahma, is called detachment. (Shankaracharya, *Vivekacūḍāmaṇi* 21)

- As long as breath dwells in the body, so long do they inquire of your welfare at home. Once the breath leaves, the body decays, and even the wife fears that very same body. (Shankaracharya, *Bhaja Govindam* 6)

- Who is your wife? Who is your son? Supremely wonderful, indeed, is this *saṁsāra*. Of whom are you? From where have you come? Oh, brother, think of that Truth here. (Shankaracharya, *Bhaja Govindam* 8)

- Through the company of the good arises nonattachment; through nonattachment arises freedom from delusion; when there is freedom from delusion, there is immutable Reality; on experiencing immutable Reality, there comes the state of liberation-in-life. (Shankaracharya, *Bhaja Govindam* 9)

- The Self is not attained through discourses nor through memorizing scriptural texts, nor through much learning. It is gained only by him who wishes to attain It with his whole heart. To such a one, the Self reveals Its true nature. (*Muṇḍaka Upaniṣad* II:3)

FURTHER READING

- Shankaracharya, *Bhaja Govindam*. Commentary by Swami Chinmayananda. Bombay: Central Chinmaya Mission Trust, 1990.

- Shankaracharya, *Vivekachoodamani* (*Vivekacūḍāmaṇi*). Commentary by Swami Chinmayananda. Bombay: Central Chinmaya Mission Trust, 1987. Verses 18-30.

Meditation 19

It is not enough to strive to understand the sacred texts, which any professor can; nor merely to feel the Truth, which any person without vision can. Understanding is developed through the study of the scriptures, and feeling for God is increased by devotion. Yet, study alone will never take us to the Truth, nor is feeling the Truth sufficient for us to realize It. Alone, neither way is enough for realizing the Truth, because the Truth lies beyond the mind. To make Truth our own, we must apprehend it directly in our own experience. It is in the seat of meditation that we learn to *use the mind to rise beyond the mind* — and realize the Truth as our own innermost Self.

The knowledge of Vedanta we have newly gained may not bless us yet because the mind that absorbed the teaching is still the old mind, filled with its old habits. In order to reap the blessings of our spiritual search we need to create a new habit in the mind, the habit of seeing our identity in the pure Self, not in the body, mind, or intellect. Again and again, we must cut our identification with the not-Self. The various paths prescribed by the great masters of the past help us in developing that habit. But in addition to following those paths — as we act without selfish desire (*karma yoga*), learn to be devoted to the Lord (*bhakti yoga*), and study the scriptures (*jñāna yoga*) — we must consciously turn the mind away from extroverted pursuits to contemplate upon the essentially blissful nature of the Self.

The mind learns to accept new habits of thinking through

the practice of meditation. In meditation, the mind dwells only on one thought, a thought that reminds us of the Lord and our own pure and limitless nature.

Preparing the Mind: *Japa*

Meditation is the subtlest of human activities and requires that our minds be fully prepared for it through the various methods of purification prescribed by the masters. The time taken for meditation is a small part of the day, while the rest of the day is employed in various activities. These activities have an influence on our meditation. If, for instance, our activities are selfish and greedy, then agitations will disturb the mind in its attempts at meditation. In contrast, disciplined and selfless actions purify the mind and make it peaceful — and ready it for meditation. Thus, in order to become effective meditators we must organize our day's activities in such a way as to prepare in the inner personality a conducive atmosphere for meditation.

Even after having prepared the mind through various methods of purification, the masters still do not advise us to dive straight into meditation, but urge us to prepare the mind first by chanting the Lord's name. New students of Vedanta, in their initial eagerness, may wonder why they should take up any *sādhanā* at all other than pure meditation. It is natural for seekers to question the importance of preparatory techniques such as *japa,* the repetition of a divine name. The masters answer this impatience of the student thus:

In *japa,* the mind is given a word symbol of the Divine (a mantra) to chant silently to itself, to the exclusion of all other thoughts. When the mind is constantly chanting a chosen mantra, it reaches a state of single-pointed attention, the beginning stage of meditation. Thus, *japa* is a training for the mind that prepares a student for meditation by bringing the mind to attend to a single-pointed focus. Without that initial preparation, the student's attempts at meditation will very likely end in dismal failure. In fact, *japa* properly done can bring about a more sustained single-pointedness of the mind than all the hasty attempts at meditation. A mind seasoned with *japa* is like preprepared food that is ready for consumption after a few short seconds of warming on the fire. A *japa*-conditioned mind can soar to unimaginable heights in meditation in a very short time.

The logic behind *japa* is simple. We cannot say a word without a thought form rising up immediately in the mind, nor can we have a thought form without its corresponding name.

> Try! Can you repeat the word *pen* without its form appearing in your mind? Try it. Can you say *lake* and not have the image of a body of water appear in your mind's eye?

This close connection between the name and the form constitutes the underlying principle of the technique called *japa*. As soon as we chant our chosen name of the Lord (a mantra), an association with Him automatically rises up in the mind.

Another important principle employed in the technique of *japa* is the fact that attachment is caused by a repetition of thought. Thoughts running continuously toward an object create an attachment to it. When our thought flow toward an object increases, our attachment to it also increases; and when we reduce our thought flow toward an object, our attachment diminishes. Then when the thought flow toward an object is completely expelled from the mind, no attachment at all remains. Thus, by continuous repetition of the name of the Lord, we get attached to Him, with a consequent detachment from the outer world of objects.

The Process

Choose a special room or a quiet corner of a room for your meditation and prayers. It is the common experience of many seekers, particularly in larger cities, not to be able to find a quiet place for meditation amid the noise both inside and outside the house. The solution is to choose a quiet time, such as early in the morning, when even the usual noisy places are silent and peaceful. But we have to keep in mind that an absolute quiet can never be found, even in the serene atmosphere of the Himalayas. In fact, real tranquillity exists only within ourselves, not in the environment.

Altar

In your place of meditation, set up an altar with your chosen image of the Lord in front of the meditation seat, with the feet of the Lord in level with the vision of your eyes. If you choose not to use an image of the Lord, place an image of *Om* (ॐ) in front of your meditation seat. Flowers, incense, and other decorations can help suggest to the sense organs that the mind is about to withdraw from the world and enter a contemplative mood.

Seat and Posture

Place a thin, flat cushion or a blanket folded into four on the floor in front of your altar. If sitting in a legs-folded position is uncomfortable for you, sit on a chair, with your back straight and not supported by the back of the chair. Thus, with your vertebral column erect, slightly bending forward at the pelvic region, place your left hand on your left thigh and your right hand, which is holding a *mala* (rosary), near the right knee. Look at the image of the Lord on your altar and take it in with love. Then gently close your eyes, looking nowhere in particular.

Thought Massage

Now start your "thought massage" to relax the body: With your mind, slowly tap the various muscles of the body, starting from the head and descending to the toes. Let the mind inspect the muscles, urging them to release their stiffness and tension. When the thought massage is complete, you have successfully withdrawn your attention from the disturbances of the physical body.

Thought Parade

The next source of disturbance is the mind, in which the predominant thoughts and desires of the day rise up and cause agitations. Let these thoughts rise spontaneously to the surface and exhaust themselves. Do not suppress them, but let them express themselves and pass away. As you do so, do not initiate any fresh thoughts or attach yourself to any thought being expressed. As the thoughts pass before you, post your intellect as a detached witness of the rising and passing away of thoughts. The intellect acts as a commanding officer in an army parade when he takes the salute and watches the proceedings without identifying with any one soldier parading before him. By this process, called the "thought parade," all agitations in your mind will subside, at least temporarily, and your mind will become available for *japa*.

Chanting the Mantra

Start to chant your chosen mantra in the mind as you visualize the divine symbol on your altar, invoking feelings of love and surrender. To keep your mind fixed on the mantra, turn the beads of your mala with each chant. The Hindu *mala* consists of 108 beads strung together on a cord, with a small space between each bead and with the off-bead, the *meru*, jutting out from the string of beads.

With your right hand take your *mala* and search for the off-bead. Bring the tips of your thumb and the ring finger together, and at that juncture hang the *mala*. Let the *mala*-holding hand rest on your knee. Repeat your mantra and, starting immediately after the *meru*, turn a bead with each repetition of the mantra. Turn each bead with your middle finger and thumb, always toward you, while keeping the index finger apart. The index finger is not employed in *japa* since it represents duality, being the finger we use to point out the otherness of things and to accuse and threaten others.

When you have repeated your mantra 108 times, turning one bead with each repetition, you will have reached the *meru*. Don't cross the *meru*. Turn the beads around and start the next *mala* of *japa* on the bead you turned with the 107th mantra of the first *mala*. While chanting the mantra in your mind, let the intellect observe the chant. So long as the mind is chanting the mantra, the turning of the beads continues; when the mind strays away, the movement of the *mala* stops. This causes a jerk, bringing the mind's attention back to the chant.

After you have chanted your mantra for some time, put a sudden stop to the chanting as though someone had shouted, "Stop!" The order to stop must come from within you. If you find this difficult, continue chanting louder and louder in your mind. When you have reached the peak, slowly and steadily reduce the volume until your mental chant is a mere whisper. Then allow the whisper of your mantra to dissolve into a positive silence within. When you have moved into a thoughtless state for a split moment, hold on to it as long as you can. As soon as thoughts rise up from the silence, chant your mantra to help move you into the thoughtless state once again. Repeat this process as many as three times during one sitting. However, remember never to strain and force the mind to do more than it can do with ease, and never force it to hold the silence longer than it can. If you try to elongate the silence by force, you will create suppressions, which can only hamper your spiritual unfoldment.

Thus, for a few sweet moments, cheerfully learn to halt the mind from all its usual wanderings in the realm of objects, emotions, and thoughts. Under such balmy quiet, a lacerated mind becomes revitalized and refills itself with a new power. In quietude, the mind can bring forth new ideals, solutions, and endlessly creative ideas. At such moments of inner tranquillity, the mind can reach out to profound thoughts that are ordinarily too high for us to grasp readily. When we are still, then alone the infinite resources of the Total Mind flow down to flood our inner selves.

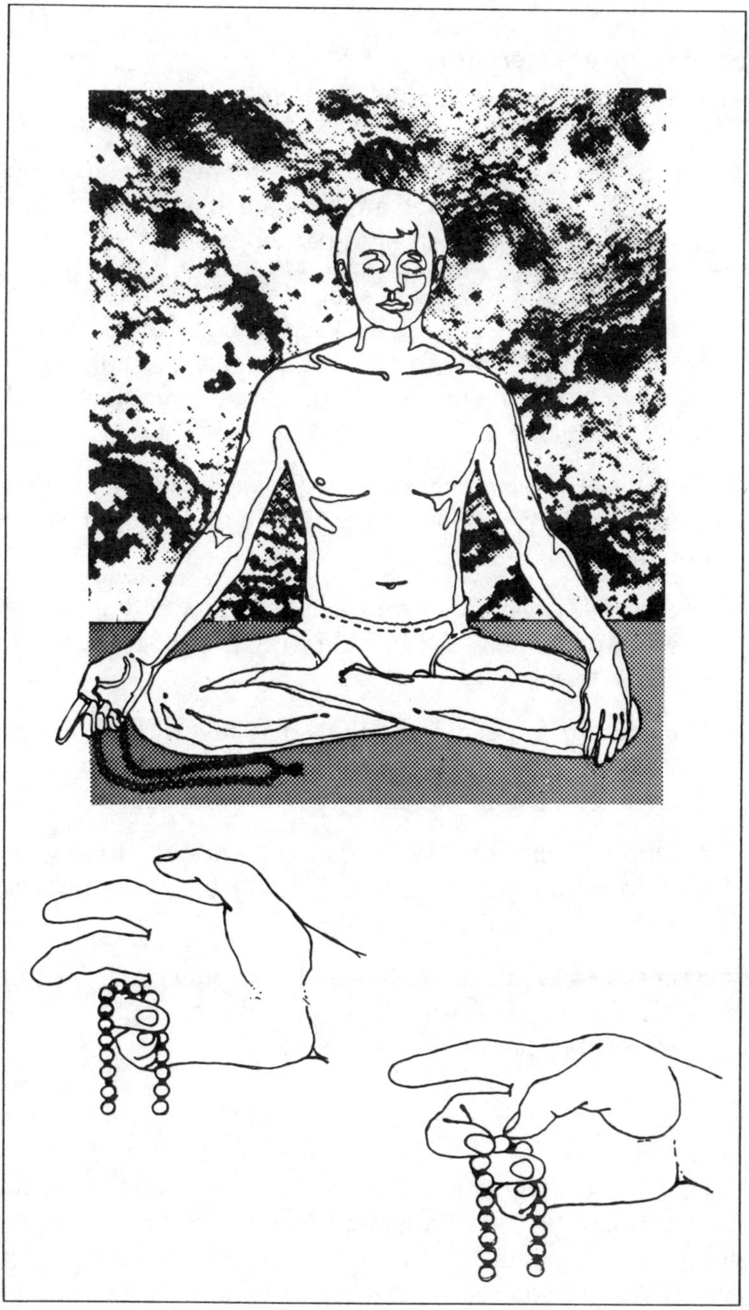

Summary of Procedure

To summarize the meditation procedure:

1. *Seat.* Set aside a special room or place for meditation. Sit on a flat cushion or a folded blanket on the floor. If you cannot sit on the floor, use a straight-backed chair.
2. *Posture.* Sit on the floor in a legs-folded position or on a chair with your back straight. Keep your vertebral column erect, leaning slightly forward at the pelvic region. Keep your left hand on your left thigh and let your right hand rest, holding the *mala*, on your right knee.
3. *Contemplating your symbol of the Divine.* Fix your gaze on your chosen symbol of the Lord and surrender to Him in devotion.
4. *Thought massage.* Close your eyes and mentally massage every part of your body, starting with the head and ending with the toes.
5. *Thought parade.* Let any thoughts that have already arisen in your mind parade in front of you as you watch them in detachment. Do not initiate any new thoughts.
6. *Chanting by the mind.* With your eyes closed, chant your mantra in your mind while turning the beads of the *mala*. Watch your mind chanting.
7. *Thoughtless state.* Suddenly stop the mental chanting and watch the silence within. If you find this difficult, resume your mental chanting.

For some temperaments, the morning hours are best for meditation. For others, perhaps because of the program of their life's duties, late evenings are most suitable. Some prefer moonlit nights. Others consider caves the best place for quieting the mind. Still others find a field under the open sky the most conducive place to meditate. In fact, these external factors of time and place have nothing to do with the practice of meditation, but students in their initial attempts do receive psychological help from such factors. The scriptures, too, encourage them.

After discovering through trial and error the best hour and place for meditation, decide to pursue your meditative practice systematically. In the beginning, sit down for meditation only ten minutes at a time. With even a ten-minute conscious rest of the mind, you can revive it from all its fatigue and recharge it with new vitality. Conscious rest is the secret of mental revitalization.

Mantras

A mantra is a word symbol expressing a particular view of God and the universe. The sampling of mantras that follows provides you with choices for your own *japa* practice:

Vedantic Mantras

Tat tvam asi	That thou art.
Aham Brahmāsmi	I am *Brahman*.
Ayam Ātmā Brahma	This Self is *Brahman*.
Śivoham, Śivoham	I am Shiva, auspiciousness.
Tadeva Satyam Tad Brahma	That alone is Truth; That is *Brahman*.
Ānandoham, Ānandoham	I am *ānanda*, I am bliss.
Hamsaḥ Soham, Soham Hamsaḥ	I am He, He am I; He am I, I am He.

Puranic Mantras

Om Namo Nārāyaṇāya
Om Śrī Rāma, Jaya Rāma, Jaya, Jaya Rāma
Om Namaḥ Śivāya
Om Śrī Ṣaṇmukhāya Namaḥ
Om Śrī Rāmacandrāya Namaḥ
Om Śrī Lakṣmyai Namaḥ

Cautions

The mind has a tendency to drift away repeatedly from the point of concentration, even while chanting a mantra. To prevent such digression and to maintain concentration, you can apply certain external aids, such as the fragrance of flowers or incense or the sound of bells. If the mind still runs away, try, again and again, to bring it back to the point of concentration.

If subjective disturbances continue to plague you, keep your eyes open and even chant your mantra out loud until the disturbances disappear and the mind gains relative poise and concentration. You can apply the same treatment when sleep tries to overcome you during *japa*.

If you are still unable to maintain your concentration in spite of these efforts, you may be overstepping your present capacity to concentrate. If so, practice concentration upon a larger field. For instance, to begin with, study the scriptures or stories about the various divine incarnations during the allotted meditation time. Thus, through study, you can develop the art of maintaining one consistent thought, that of the Divine. Later, you can introduce forms or pictures of divine beings to help you channel your thoughts in one direction. When you find yourself successful at this stage, choose to concentrate on one feature of the Lord's form, such as His face; still later, narrow your point of concentration down to the Lord's smile. Thus, stage by stage, you learn to converge your thoughts to a single-pointed focus. When you reach sufficient concentration, close your eyes again and practice chanting your mantra in the mind.

A mind that still remains unruly may at times respond to persuasion. You can try to draw the attention of the mind to the profits of concentration and the supreme benefits to be achieved through meditation. Some minds may not react to persuasion, but are curious by nature. In such cases, kindle the curiosity of the mind by inducing it to investigate the mystery of the unknown Self within. When this also fails, sometimes a little punishment is in order. You can threaten the uncooperative mind with fasting or a cold bath. Once you have enunciated your threat, do not fail to carry the promised punishment out if the mind persists in disobeying you; however, be careful not to carry this treatment too far, and use it only as a last recourse.

Yet another practical way of controlling a rambling mind is to let the intellect witness the pranks of the mind, just as though it were a disobedient child. After trying all the means of controlling such a child, an intelligent mother tries the method of disinterestedly witnessing his mischievous deeds. The child invariably feels uneasy at her silent reproach and quietly returns to her care. Similarly, when the mind realizes that the intellect is watching it, it becomes self-conscious and ashamed and returns to the control of the intellect.

The Final Stages

The last stage of contemplative practice is meditation (*dhyāna*). When the seeker has succeeded in keeping his single-pointed concentration for a prolonged period of time, he is ready to enter the state of thoughtlessness (*samādhi*).

As long as the mind is engaged in chanting the Lord's name, the mind and intellect are still active. As you step up the concentrated spell of chanting and then suddenly stop to experience the silence of the mind, there is now neither the mind nor the intellect. That moment of dynamic silence is the peace inherent in your pure Self. In its purest form, meditation at this juncture is a point at which the meditator, the meditated, and the meditation all merge into One.

The Self in each one of us is the supreme Consciousness that pervades all of life. It is like the sun reflected in a pool of water. When the water in the pool is disturbed, the sun's reflection is not seen; when it is steady and calm, the reflection becomes visible. Similarly, pure Consciousness is reflected in the "thought pool," the mind. If agitations exist in the mind, the reflection of Consciousness cannot be seen. However, when the agitations cease and the mind becomes peaceful and calm, the Self reveals Itself. At this point, the meditator reaches the state called *samādhi,* which literally means "tranquil mind."

As we have already seen, the Self is known in three states: the waking, the dream, and the deep sleep states.[1] These states can be represented in the three sounds that comprise *Om*: *A, U,* and *M.* The sound *A* represents the waking state; the sound *U* represents the dream state; and the sound *M* represents the deep-sleep state. The waking state is superimposed on the *A* sound because it is the first of the three states of consciousness, and the sound *A* is the first letter in the alphabet, in any language. The dream state occurs between the waking and the deep-sleep states and is thus second among the three states of consciousness. Since *U* is the sound between *A* and *M*, it is used to represent the middle state, the dream state. The sound *M* represents deep sleep in that it is the closing sound of the syllable, just as deep sleep is the final stage of the mind at rest.

A short, pregnant silence is inevitable between two successive utterings of *Om*. This silence represents yet another state, the fourth, called *Turīya* in Sanskrit. This is the state of perfect bliss when the individual self recognizes its identity with the Supreme. In fact, the silence of *Turīya* is the very substratum upon which the three sounds *A-U-M* are built. And when the sounds are no longer uttered, what remains is pure, undisturbed silence. We may consider, therefore, that the three sounds emerge out of silence, exist in silence, and merge back into silence again. Similarly, pure Consciousness remains ever preset. The three states of consciousness (waking, dream, and deep sleep) emerge out of Consciousness, exist in Consciousness, and finally merge back into Consciousness. When we transcend these three states, we realize the pure Self.

Self-realization is often described as occurring in two stages. In the initial stage of realization, the last trace of individuality lingers only to experience Godhood. This state

[1] Discussed in Chapter 14, "Three Worlds."

is called *savikalpa samādhi*. The second stage of realization is called *nirvikalpa samādhi*. In this stage, the last trace of individuality, which had previously claimed realization, itself merges with the Infinite. What remains thereafter is only *Brahman*, the one supreme Reality.

Through repeated practice of meditation, the mind learns to abide in the blissful silence of the Self and own up the knowledge it has assumed through study. When the extroverted mind disappears in the silence of the pure Self, the merger is complete. As the great Vedantin Sri Shankaracharya describes it, the merger is as water mixing with water, light combining with light, and space merging with space. In each of these examples, the merger not only creates a homogeneity, but also leaves not a trace of recognition of the separateness that existed before the merger. Similarly, in meditation, the identity of the individuality is lost in the experience of the Self, which is one with *Brahman*, unlimited Consciousness.

Tips for Success

Regularity and sincerity are the secrets of success in meditation. Go slowly; allow the momentum of meditation to lift you into it. Evolution is not a matter of hurry-burry. Meditation is not a question of dashing into the divine silence; let it come to you. We can never dash into sleep, can we? We prepare ourselves for sleep and then invoke it. Sleep comes in its own rhythm and envelops us.

Everything in Nature is slow and steady — except for earthquakes and storms, which are destructive.

> The opening of a flower, the germination of a seed, the growth of a tree, the sunrise and the moonrise, the high tide and the low tide — all are slow processes, though they are precisely timed. If you sit near the sea and watch, you will find how slowly and steadily the waves rise and fall; how rhythmic it all is. There are no jerks. In the same way, you cannot dash into the presence of the Lord. You cannot force your entry.

If silence does not easily envelop you during meditation,

do not despair. The spiritual life is meant for the imperfect, not the perfect. The seeker who condemns himself for his imperfections is a fool. He does not know what he is doing: He is unintelligently meditating upon his own negative qualities and imperfections, and therefore his imperfections become more and more pronounced. Instead, surrender your imperfections to the Lord.

When we offer fruits and flowers to our spiritual teacher, we are symbolically surrendering our imperfections to him. Flowers are the source of fragrance, and that fragrance is symbolic of our *vāsanās*. When we offer flowers, we are symbolically offering up our *vāsanās*. When we offer fruits, we are offering the fruits of our actions. By thus offering up the *vāsanās* that block us from the Divine and by surrendering our attachment to the results of our actions, symbolized by the fruit, we are making ourselves available for the Lord to cure us of our imperfections.

This attempt at surrender leads to the highest mood of meditation. An emotional person who surrenders to the beloved Lord of his heart reaches the same mood of meditation as the intellectual one, who, after he has understood that the Consciousness illumining everything is his own pure Self, turns away from the external world to dive deep into the blissful serenity within.

By thus surrendering the bundle of your futile memories of the past and your worries about the future at His feet, rest in a mood of cheer. Rich in a faith born of understanding, learn to smile away your sorrows. Be unaffected by the play of *sattva, rajas,* and *tamas* in you. With such a cheerful mind, you can transform the subtle equipment within you and prepare it for the meditative flight. Meditation should not be ordered by the clock on the wall or the position of the sun in the sky. Instead, it should depend upon the cheer and vigor in the mind.

Never give up. Strive on. Regularity and sincerity will take you to your goal. Spiritual unfoldment is reserved for the wise heroes.

For Your Study and Reflection

19. Meditation

STUDY QUESTIONS, Level 1

1. Why during the thought parade should you not let yourself identify with any of the thoughts you see parading in front of you?

2. Why should you not force your mind to meditate longer than it can with ease?

3. Outline the seven steps of the meditation procedure; be sure to include the preparatory steps.

STUDY QUESTIONS, Level 2

1. Describe the logic behind *japa*. How does *japa* help focus the mind?

2. How can the power of concentration you develop through your meditative practice help you in everyday life? Give examples of how concentration helps lead to success in various endeavors.

3. Why is an attitude of surrender conducive to success in meditation? *What* do you surrender?

FOR YOUR REFLECTION

- Let the yogi try constantly to keep the mind steady, remaining in solitude, with the mind and body controlled, free from hope and greed. (*Bhagavad Gītā* V:10)

- Thus, always keeping the mind balanced, the yogi, with his mind controlled, attains to the peace abiding in Me, which culminates in total liberation. (*Bhagavad Gītā* V:15)

- When the perfectly controlled mind rests in the Self only, free from longing for all objects of desire, then it is said, "It is united." (*Bhagavad Gītā* V:18)

- I am without attributes and actions; eternal (*nitya*); without any desire and thought (*nirvikalpa*); without any dirt (*nirañjana*); without any change (*nirvikāra*); without form (*nirākāra*); ever liberated (*nitya mukta*); ever pure (*nirmala*). (Shankaracharya, *Ātma Bodha* 34)

FURTHER READING

- Swami Chinmayananda, *Meditation and Life*. Piercy, California: Chinmaya Publications West, 1992.

Sustained Joy 20

When you want to tame any animal or persuade another individual to do his job, it is always necessary that you put that animal or individual in a happy mood first. When the person is in a happy mood, you can easily get your job done through him — but not when he is preoccupied or mentally worried. The principle is:

The mind is available for remolding when it is in a cheerful, happy mood.

This cheerful, happy mood is the beginning trace of *sattva*, serenity.

Persuading the Mind

As a meditator, you are trying to persuade your own mind, not anyone outside. You are trying to persuade it to engage in contemplation of the Higher, and the mind will be easily available for your purpose when it is in a happy, cheerful mood. Though bliss is your true nature, and even though you are always searching for happiness in all of your efforts, your mind is at this moment addicted to sorrow.

Even in a happy situation, you and I are afraid to be too happy. That is our nature now — out of sheer habit. The majority of us consider that to be happy or cheerful is to be irresponsible in life. We think that to be in tension, under severe stress and strain, is our normal condition.

Many of you will have to persuade yourselves in the beginning to learn the art of being cheerful within, especially when you sit for meditation. In that happy mood, the mind is plastic; you can then reshape its contours and get out of it a better performance. Not only during the time of meditation, but also in your outside activities, in the long run, a healthy and cheerful mind will produce a better performance. In a happy mood, much of the mind's crookedness is straightened; its unsymmetrical development is transformed into symmetrical beauty.

The mind of a master is much more glorious than his mind was before he reached those peaks. With such a trained and beautified mind, he contacts the external world. When you possess such a trained mind, even though you are in the midst of sense objects, problems, and challenges, you are not in the least perturbed. And when the mind is not perturbed, your vision is not clouded. You go through life gathering no moss. You maintain your mind — your divine beauty and purity — immaculate.

In order to mold the mind into that beauty and purity, the present mind needs to be readjusted. And when you systematically and correctly meditate, that readjustment begins to take place. Among the very first signposts to show that you are on the right path is the gathering joy within, a stability and poise in spite of problems you may meet outside. And in all such conditions, the spiritual student generally misunderstands the new mood; he becomes afraid that he may be developing a sense of irresponsibility in the world. It is not so. The joys of the world do not excite him. The sorrows of the world come to him, jeer at him; yet, he feels untouched by them. Seekers often ask, "What is happening to me? My brother died, and I am not upset. Before, such a situation was sufficient to upset me for a whole year; now it doesn't affect me. Have I become dead inside?" This kind of a doubt may come to the mind. It is not a sign of irresponsibility or numbness. It is a sign of your inner growth.

After you've set up your meditation room or corner, try to use the same place every day. Slowly, that room, that corner, that seat will gather an atmosphere of its own. It will become a psychological harbor for you. By association of ideas, the moment you sit there, your mind will automatically become quiet. In that quietude, move your mind into a cheerful mood. Smile away — not with your lips but in your mind. Within a short time, after a few days of conscious effort, at a moment's notice and under any circumstance, you will be able to change the mood in your mind to this attitude of inner joy. Repeating your mantra helps bring that attitude back to your mind.

All great masters, saints, and sages constantly live in this attitude of joy. And it is this cheerful mood that we see in their eyes, an enchantment of peace and joy. Just as a miserable person throws a dark, dreary, and tragic atmosphere around him, a peaceful and happy master spreads an atmosphere of joy, so that even when the grossest of us come near him, we become filled with some mysterious, voiceless experience that generates a spirit of reverence toward him.

Only in that cheerful atmosphere of the mind can spirituality develop. That is the reason why many devotees go to the church, mosque, temple, or other place of worship. They go there with all their sorrows and kneel and weep and pray for hours together. But many make the mistake of allowing the mind to stay loaded down with its sorrows. Even after years of prayer, such minds develop more of an attitude of tragedy than a satisfying mood of joy.

So when you go to your seat of meditation, bring the mind to a mood of joy.

> Even today, when you have ten minutes to yourself, sit down and practice smiling in your mind. Don't smile with your lips, just with your mind. Watch what happens. It doesn't matter if your eyes remain open. Simply watch the mind and make it smile; drop all of its worries for the time being.

You'll see that in a cheerful mind, very few agitations rise up. And in a mind with minimum agitations, *sattva* predominates.

Surrender

In your daily meditation, you need not follow each and every one of the various methods and strategies by which you can persuade the mind to come to quietude. Each day your mind will bring a different weapon, and from your armory you must select the right weapon as an antidote. On certain days, for example, you will feel a special attachment to the body. By relaxing the body, to a large extent your attachment to it will be temporarily released.

Thereafter, the mind's source of disturbance — the ego and all its anxieties — is bound to make its showing. Don't curse yourself; anxieties are natural. They come to you because of your relationships. In yourself, there is no worry. Because of the relationships pertaining to your field of activities, disturbances reach your mind.

Surrender your anxieties at the feet of the Lord or the teacher. When you are surrendering unto Him, surrender all your roles. You are no longer a mother now, nor a student, son, father, daughter, boss, or professional. Renounce every attitude that you have taken in your relationship with the world of objects, emotions, and thoughts through your body, mind, and intellect. At such a moment, you are nothing, You, the created, are turning toward your Creator. He and you are alone; it is a private interview:

> "O Lord, this is all your *māyā* only. I know You are just behind the very sorrow I am now facing. . . . Apart from You, I don't exist. Everything in me is already laid at Your feet. . . . I am neither mother, daughter, or worker in the office. O Lord, all that I am is Yours alone."

When you are thus dead to all other relationships, all worries and responsibilities drop away. Only you and the Divine are present. Your mind is flooded in joy because you are turning toward your Beloved. Think of it this way:

> "I have an appointment with God. I am turning toward my

own Source. I am temporarily leaving behind all the fields of pain and imperfection."

As soon as the meditation is over, take your responsibilities on your shoulders again.

Invoke floods of joy in your mind, and from your mind let your joy spread in every direction. With every cell in your body radiate this joy. As this mood increases in the mind, the mind becomes filled with *sattva*. And a serene mind is the most effective instrument of contemplation. When the mind is in that serene attitude, the body is relaxed, because your entire attention goes to the point of joy. With this mind, chant the Lord's name. Be aware of the chant. Then gradually slow down the chanting. Since your attention has been on the chanting, your mind has rolled away from all objects outside; it has become extremely introverted. When the chanting is removed, what remains is your true nature alone. There try to remain: "I am."

All that you have studied and reflected on in the scriptures — whether in the Bible, the Koran, the Torah, the Dhammapada, or the Upanishads — all those ideas will help give you an understanding of your true nature. Try to remain in that quietude, vigilantly conscious of that quiet. Assert in yourself: "I am. This Self is *Brahman*."

Make it your habit to keep the mind in this attitude of inner tranquillity. The external world will always be full of contentions, conflicts, and sorrows — everything changing at every moment. It is made that way; it should be so. Known factors clash; unknown factors appear. This is the nature of the world. But in your inner poise *you* have control, and you can keep that control.

If you assume unnecessary mental worries, you only create more problems outside and become more incompetent to face them. To move away from your inner tranquillity is to sink to the animal level where there is no dignity for the human being. By its old habit, the mind will again try to tumble into imagined sorrows, remembered worries, and fancied problems of the future — it goes on. Refuse to come down from the peak of inner joy. Sport in any problems you encounter. In the struggle of life, the one who has this inner poise always wins.

Invocation of the Higher

As you continue your meditative practice, you will learn to withdraw more and more from the sense appetites and the anxiety to hoard. Your daily *sādhanā* will deepen in ardor, broaden in love, expand to touch new realms of spiritual experience. You will find greater pleasure in your daily prayers and gradually come to understand that the very environment in which the Lord has placed you is the most conducive one for your growth. With this understanding in the heart, you are ready to wade through the muddy pools of life while constantly remembering Him.

However, be ever watchful whether you might be slipping from your peak of joy. Learn to rediscover the joyous mood even while moving about, while talking to others. Even when failures from all sides grin at you, remain ever drunk in your own joy.

Still if times do come when you find yourself empty, exhausted, and once again in the grips of your lower nature, remember the advice of the sages: Invoke the Lord and rediscover your association with Him:

> *Always, free from all mental anxiety, invoke the Lord and seek Him alone — with all factors of your personality.* (*Nārada Bhakti Sūtra* VIII:2:79)

We fall back into our lower nature when the mind reverts to its old habits of thought and feels cut off from the Higher. At such times, reestablish your connection with the Divine. Surrender to the Lord. Invoke Him. Your invocation must be an outpouring of all your faculties as you glorify Him Who dwells within you. At the physical, mental, and intellectual levels, be ready to put forth all the best in you as an offering to Him. Let your actions sing His glory. Let your feelings waft the fragrance of His eternal purity. Let your thoughts pour out, expressing His dynamism and divine will.

When your whole being is centered in ardent invocation of the Higher, you are gradually transformed — and discover that you attain the very attributes you are worshipping. As you invoke Him and contemplate upon His glories, your mind is cut loose from its fanciful attachments to the pluralistic world. The sorrows and worries that may have brought about your temporary "fall" are now lifted to reveal glimpses of the blissful nature of your higher Self.

Truth is not anything separate from you; it is already present as the illuminator behind every thought you think. As soon as the mind is hushed, Truth is uncovered.

> You have lost your house key, and you look for it for a long time in futile excitement. At last, you discover it in your own pocket! The key was always there, but not being aware of its presence, you searched in vain for it everywhere.
>
> Truth is with us all the time, but we do not know it. When we invoke It, we experience It as a divine revelation.

To rediscover the Truth that was always in us but had become temporarily veiled is the culmination of evolution. As you rediscover the truth of your own nature, the pure Self, you gain an unshakeable peace and a never-ending joy. Recognition of the Self is the crowning victory in life. This is *Īśvara darśana*, "the vision of God." Once you own that vision, no outer circumstance — of sorrow or joy, insult or respect, failure or success, poverty or riches, disaster or progress — can touch you. You are above all circumstances. You are no longer a victim of the external, but are ever rooted in your realization of the pure Self, which is the Self everywhere. You become a calm witness of the universe, as if it were a mere temporary disturbance within the great expanse of yourself!

For Your Study and Reflection

20. Sustained Joy

STUDY QUESTIONS, Level 1

1. Why can we say that a cardinal attitude in Vedanta is "Refuse to weep; keep smiling"? Why is such an attitude important in one's spiritual search?

2. How does the regular practice of meditation help break old habit patterns?

3. What do you think it means to "invoke the Lord"?

STUDY QUESTIONS, Level 2

1. Give examples from your daily life of how with a joyous mind it was easier to solve difficult problems. What qualities of a worried or sorrowful mind stand in the way of efficient work or problem-solving?

2. How do you think a cheerful mind is a sign of *sattva*?

3. The scriptures often remind us that surrender is an important quality for the spiritual student to cultivate. How does surrender help a seeker in his quest?

FOR YOUR REFLECTION

- No worry or anxiety should be entertained at worldly losses, as it is the nature of a true devotee to surrender constantly his limited self and all its secular and sacred activities to the Lord of his heart. (*Nārada Bhakti Sūtra* VI:2:61)

- When invoked, He, indeed, reveals Himself and makes the devotee realize His absolute nature divine. (*Nārada Bhakti Sūtra* IX:1:80)

- Tranquillity is the innate nature of all; it is a self-existent reality. Therefore, there need be no striving to produce it. Abolish agitation, and tranquillity reveals itself. Effort is needed not to generate tranquillity but to banish agitation. The mass of light, the sun's disc, is concealed by clouds. The clouds only need move away, and immediately the solar disc, which appeared to be nonexistent, reveals itself. Here there is no question of producing the solar disc and making it shine forth. In the same way, with the cessation of agitation, tranquillity rises forth. (Swami Tapovanam, *Wanderings in the Himalayas*, page 166)

FURTHER READING

- *Nārada Bhakti Sūtra*. Commentary by Swami Chinmayananda. Bombay: Central Chinmaya Mission Trust, 1990.

- Swami Tapovanam, *Wanderings in the Himalayas*. Bombay: Central Chinmaya Mission Trust, 1981. Pages 166-168.

Appendix I
Hinduism

Sanātana Dharma

The Hindus call their religion *Sanātana Dharma*, "The Eternal *Dharma*." The word *dharma* has a deeper and wider meaning than the meaning of the word *religion* as generally understood by those who use it. The word *dharma* comes from the Sanskrit root *dhṛ*, which means "to hold" or "to support." Therefore, *dharma* stands for that which holds up or supports the existence of a thing. Everything in the whole universe has its own *dharma* because it must rely on something for its existence. And what is that on which the existence of a thing depends? It is the essential nature of a thing without which it cannot exist. The essential nature of a thing is, therefore, called *dharma*. For example, fire burns; its power of burning is its *dharma*.

Divinity, Our Essential Nature

A human being also has an essential nature that upholds his existence as distinct from the rest of creation. That essential nature must be his *dharma*. So naturally we ask: What is this essential nature, or *dharma*, of a human? The Hindus strongly and emphatically uphold that the *dharma* of a human being is his capacity to become divine, which distinguishes him from all other beings. This declaration may leave one stunned; the believers of certain religions may even take the statement as heretical and blasphemous. "How can a human being become divine?" they may ask.

The equally startling reply is: "Because divinity is already in us!" This confident statement may startle, disgust, and frighten many people. But why should it? This truth has been clearly stated in all the major scriptures of the world. To give some examples from the Bible:

1. In the Book of Genesis, we are informed that before God created the world, there was nothing except God. And God has often been described as omnipresent, omnipotent, and omniscient. If God is omnipresent — meaning that He is present everywhere and that there is no place where He is not — does it not stand to reason that everything else is pervaded by Him, that He is in everyone and in everything?

The word *creation* as used in Genesis may give us a wrong idea because *to create* implies the production of a new form with a new name from some existing raw material. If only God existed before the Creation, then He must have been the raw material from which all the forms and names sprang. In Hinduism, "creation" is not the production of new forms from something nonexistent but the "projection" from what existed before Creation took place. Since only God existed before the Creation, then the whole world and every member of the plant, animal, and human species can only be projections of the one infinite God. Hence, the human being has divinity in him; it is his very *dharma*.

2. "The Kingdom of God is within you" plainly tells of the divine in the human.

3. "Love your neighbor as yourself." Vedanta says: "You *are* your neighbor." We are divine by nature, but the divinity lies very deep within us. We do not perceive it because of our unclean minds, which stand in the way. Just as the smoke veils the flame or the dust covers the mirror, making the image on the mirror unclean, God cannot be seen through the barrier of an unclean mind. But God is there all the time — in us and everywhere. If we wish to see the light of the flame or the image in the mirror, we must clean the chimney of all the soot or the mirror of its dusty veil. Similarly, we must cleanse the mind of the impurities that veil the

divine in us. Once those impurities are cleansed, we are united through our divinity with the rest of creation; we are one with our neighbors and therefore love them as ourselves.

The Sacred Books of the Hindus

The holy texts that contain the teachings about *Sanātana Dharma* are known as the *śāstras*. *Śāstras* provide the answers to such questions as:

- Who is God?
- Where does God dwell?
- What is God like?
- How are we related to God?
- Why should we strive to reach Him?

The *śāstras* also teach us the methods by which we may realize Him; how we can bring out the divinity in us; what the obstacles are on the way; how to get over those obstacles; how we should behave or conduct ourselves; what acts we should perform; and what acts we should avoid.

Throughout the march of centuries, countless sages have reached the final goal of religion by realizing God. Many of those sages reached the same goal by treading different paths. This is one of the reasons for the numerous *śāstras* in Hinduism, which prescribe various paths to the same goal. Moreover, since it has been necessary to explain religion to different people of different capabilities and inclinations, Hinduism has given rise to different grades or types of *śāstras*, such as the *Śruti*, the *Smṛti*, the *Purāṇas*, and so on.[1]

The sacred books of the Hindus can be divided into two main categories: *Śruti* (revealed knowledge) and *Smṛti* (the practical application of eternal principles). These two categories are further subdivided thus:

[1] See Chapter 15, "Vedanta."

ŚRUTI

Four Vedas (*Ṛg, Yajur, Sāma, Atharva*)

Karma Kāṇḍa
- *Saṁhitās* (Mantras)
- *Brāhmaṇas* (Rituals)

Jñāna Kāṇḍa
- *Āraṇyakas* (Methods of worship)
- *Upaniṣads* (Vedanta)

SMṚTI

Itihāsas
- *Rāmāyaṇa*
- *Mahābhārata*

Purāṇas
- 18 Main *Purāṇas*
- 46 *Upa Purāṇas*

Dharma Śāstras
- 18 *Smṛtis*
- *Manu Smṛti*

Ṣad Darśanas
- *Nyāya* by Gautama
- *Vaiśeṣika* by Kanada
- *Sānkhya* by Kapila
- *Yoga* by Patanjali
- *Mīmāṁsā* by Jaimini
- *Vedānta* by Veda Vyasa (*Brahma Sūtras*)

Vedāṅgas
- *Śikṣa* (Phonetics)
- *Kalpa* (Religious rites)
- *Vyākaraṇa* (Grammar)

Nirukta (Vedic Glossary)
Chandas (Prosody)
Jyotiṣa (Astronomy and Astrology)

Upa Vedas
Ayurveda (Science of Life, Medicine)
Dhanur Veda (Science of Warfare)
Gandharva Veda (Science and Art of Music)
Sthāpatya Śāstra (Mechanics and Construction)

Six Schools of Philosophy

In Hinduism the word *darśana*, "vision of Truth," is used to indicate philosophy. Hinduism encompasses six schools of philosophy, called *Ṣad Darśanas* (*ṣad* means "six"). Two different classifications of the schools of Hindu philosophy are recognized by the orthodox and heterodox thinkers. The orthodox classification of the schools is:

1. *Vaiśeṣika* (Kanada)
2. *Nyāya* (Gautama)
3. *Nir-Īśvara-Sānkhya* (Kapila)
4. *Sa-Īśvara-Sānkhya* (Patanjali)
5. *Pūrva Mīmāṁsā* (Jaimini)
6. *Uttara Mīmāṁsā* (Vedanta)

The other classification, which gives equal status to the atheistic schools, is:

1. Materialism (Charvaka)
2. Buddhism (Buddha)
3. Jainism (Mahavir)
4. *Tarka* (Kanada and Gautama)
5. *Sānkhya* (Kapila and Patanjali)
6. *Pūrva Mīmāṁsā* (Jaimini) and *Uttara Mīmāṁsā* (Vedanta)

Knowledge falls into two categories: secular knowledge and spiritual knowledge.

Secular knowledge pertains to the world of things and beings. Spiritual knowledge deals with the subjective realization of the transcendental Reality that lies beyond the limitations of the phenomenal world. The theme of each of the philosophies is an inquiry into spiritual knowledge.

Spiritual knowledge is divided into two main groups: theistic and atheistic.

Theists are those who accept the Vedas and believe in an eternal Reality. The Theistic school can be classified under two categories:

1. Theistic Theism
2. Theistic Atheism

Theistic Theism accepts the Vedas and also believes in *Brahman*, the nondual eternal Truth. Pure Theistic Theism is enunciated in the *Brahma Sūtras*, which consist of the very essence of the Upanishads. This school of thought is known as *Uttara Mīmāṁsā*, which had fallen into obscurity until Adi Shankaracharya revived it and brought it to the attention of the thinkers of the world as Advaita Vedanta.

Theistic Atheism supports a belief in the Vedic declarations but not in the one eternal Truth, or *Brahman*, as indicated by the Upanishads. Followers of this school believe that the Truth cannot be realized by study, reflection, and meditation upon the Upanishadic declarations. Three main schools of Theistic Atheism exist: *Tarka, Sānkhya,* and *Pūrva Mīmāṁsā.*

The *Tarka* school follows the points of view expounded by Kanada and Gautama, whose philosophies are called *Vaiśeṣika* and *Nyāya*, respectively.

The *Sānkhyan* philosophy is most rational, analytical, and scientific in its treatment. The *Sānkhyans* fall into two groups, sustained by two great exponents, Kapila and Patanjali. Kapila's philosophy, called *Nir-Īśvara-Sānkhya*, does not take into consideration the concept of a Creator, or *Īśvara*. Patanjali introduces the concept of a Creator (*Īśvara*) in his doctrine called *Sa-Īśvara-Sānkhya*.

Pūrva ("earlier") *Mīmāṁsā* ("sequence of logical thinking") is the last in the category of Theistic Atheism. The Vedas are divided into two sections, the *Karma Kāṇda* and the *Jñāna Kāṇda*. *Karma Kāṇda* is the earlier section, which is seemingly dualistic, whereas the *Jñāna Kāṇda* constitutes the later portion, which is positively nondualistic, declaring the absolute oneness of Truth. The earlier Vedic thought, contained in the *Karma Kāṇda*, was compiled by Jaimini. The philosophy of Jaimini, discussed in the *Jaimini Sūtras*, expounds the essence of *Pūrva Mīmāṁsā*. According to this philosophy, the human being has to follow faithfully the ritualistic portion of the Vedas. If he does so, he will gain infinite merit. To enjoy the fruits of such merit, the individual soul will get a chance to live for a fixed period of time in a realm of consciousness where he can experience subtler and more intense sensuous enjoyments. This temporary resort in Heaven is conceived by the followers of *Pūrva Mīmāṁsā* as the goal of existence.

The **Atheistic** school of philosophy is classified in two categories:

1. Atheistic Atheism
2. Atheistic Theism

Atheistic Atheism declares a disbelief in either the Vedas or the supreme Truth. This school is championed by some philosophers, the most important among them being Charvaka. The Materialists (*Charvakas*) believe that no higher goal than materialism is to be achieved in life, and that the human being has only to find maximum enjoyment in sensual indulgence, unrestricted by ethical or moral scruples. They believe that the human being merely exists as he is; he comes from nowhere when he is born and goes to nowhere when he dies. At death when the body is buried, everything ends.

Atheistic Theism, however, accepts a supreme Truth beyond the body and the objects of the world; however, it refutes the Vedas. The Buddhists and the Jains fall under this category. The Atheism of Buddhism sprang from Buddha's revolt against the excessive Vedic ritualism practiced during his age. Ritualism had reached a state of absurdity, and the people following it had grown to be barbarous and immoral. Buddha denied the authority for such practices and, in doing so, had to denounce the Vedic textbooks themselves.

The Jains, the followers of Mahavir, also belong to the Atheistic Theistic school. They are considered atheistic because of their nonacceptance of the Vedas. Their theistic leanings are attributed to their belief in the eternal Truth, which is permanent, perfect, and all-blissful.

Appendix II
Study Groups

After finishing reading a text such as *Self-Unfoldment*, you may have questions that remain unanswered. Or, you may have no questions to ask but yet you feel that the newly gained knowledge is not working a change for the better in your life. You may ask: "Where do I go from here? How can I get help in my spiritual practice?"

If you've had a chance to hear Swami Chinmayananda or other teachers from Chinmaya Mission speak, at the conclusion of the talks you may find yourself asking, "Swamiji, when will you be coming again? I want to know more, but where do I go from here?" Vedanta, the science of personality rehabilitation, cannot be handed over from the lecture podium or through the pages of a book in a matter of a few days. Like any science, it must be pursued slowly and consistently. In a few lectures or through one textbook of Vedanta, Swamiji can only show us where to start; the rest is up to us.

Swami Chinmayananda has written a number of textbooks on the fundamental principles of Vedanta, as well as detailed commentaries on the *Bhagavad Gītā*, the Upanishads, and the works of Adi Shankaracharya in a style and language comprehensive to the modern mind bent toward science and technology. With great vision, he has designed a Scheme of Study, calculated not only to bring intellectual knowledge to the student, but also to assure that the student who is ready to put in the effort can, indeed, learn the means for becoming more peaceful, happy, and integrated in his life. Swamiji has suggested that this Scheme of Study be used as the basis for study groups for interested seekers.[1]

Chinmaya Study Groups

A study group is a group of five to fifteeen people who meet regularly to discuss one of the textbooks of Vedanta. The first Chinmaya study groups began in 1953 in Madras, India. Study groups are now functioning successfully in Chinmaya Mission centers all over India and the rest of the world. Active study groups now exist in Europe, the Middle East, the Far East, Canada, Australia, and the United States.

A study group is not a lecture session where one person speaks and the rest listen. All members of the group participate equally. Members study individually the portions from a textbook that are assigned for a given week's study. They meet once a week in an informal atmosphere for an hour and a half to discuss what they have studied. A group leader (*sevak*, male; *sevikā*, female) guides the discussion and assists members in their study, helping to clear any doubts that may arise.

Chinmaya Lesson Course

Study groups have also been formed for the joint study of the Chinmaya Lesson Course, a one-year correspondence course on the fundamentals of Vedanta. During the course, the student maintains direct communication with Sandeepany Sadhanalaya (an institute of Vedantic studies in Bombay, India, founded by Swami Chinmayananda), which dispenses new lessons every two weeks by mail. Periodically, the student answers questionnaires on the lessons and returns the completed questionnaires to India for correction and comments. Doubts pertaining to the material studied that are not resolved in the study group may be included with the questionnaire for further clarification. Experience has shown

[1] See Appendix III, "Scheme of Study," "Other Books by Swami Chinmayananda," and the Bibliography.

that this course makes an ideal beginning point for new study groups because it teaches the beginner the fundamentals of Vedanta in a logical and systematic manner.

Conducting a Study Group

The location for a study group is usually the home of one of the members of the group. The space must be spotlessly clean and orderly. The fragrance of incense helps create a conducive atmosphere. An altar with images or symbols of the Divine, plus a lamp or a candle, can further enhance the atmosphere for spiritual study. The group sevak usually sits near the altar.

The host needs to provide space near the door, so that members may remove their footwear before entering the study area.

The group sevak is responsible for explaining all administrative details regarding choice of text, assignments for study, time of meeting, and the importance of regularity and punctuality.

Before beginning the study, the sevak generally leads the group in chanting an invocation:

Om
Sahanāvavatu
Saha nau bhunaktu
Saha vīryam karavāvahai
Tejasvināvadhītamastu
Mā vidviṣavahai
Om, śāntiḥ, śāntiḥ, śāntiḥ

Om. May He protect us both.
May He cause us both to enjoy the Supreme.
May we both exert together (to discover the true inner meaning of the scriptures).
May our studies be thorough and brilliant.
May we never misunderstand each other.
Om, peace, peace, peace.

As the discussion of the assigned text begins, the sevak, or a group member assigned by him, briefly summarizes the previous week's lesson. Then, the first member assigned to a given portion of the text summarizes that portion for the group and comments on it. The other group members then add their own comments and interpretations, drawing parallel ideas from other books to supplement the topic under discussion. The sevak keeps the discussion on the subject and also helps clear any doubts that may arise. Members take turns summarizing the portions assigned to them until that week's assignments are finished. The sevak then assigns the portions to be studied for the next session.

The session ends with a peace invocation and/or a short meditation. The following is an invocation that may be used:

Sarve bhavantu sukhinaḥ
Sarve santu nirāmayāḥ
Sarve bhadrāṇi paśyantu
Mā kaścit duḥkha bhāg bhavet
Om, śāntiḥ, śāntiḥ, śāntiḥ

May all be happy.
May all be healthy.
May all see auspiciousness.
May none suffer.
Om, peace, peace, peace.

Questions about Study Groups

Q: *Who can join a study group?*

A: Anyone over 16 years of age, with intellectual acumen and an aspiration to rediscover his or her own divine nature.

Q: *I don't have much time. What can I do?*

A: If you try, you will surely be able to spare 90 minutes out of one week for yourself. Doctors, engineers, lawyers, business magnates, students, and many others, all with very busy lives, attend study groups regularly. All have thereby become better at whatever they do, whether in their professional lives or at home.

Q: *Is it necessary to know the Sanskrit language?*

A: No, it is not necessary. However, some familiarity with Sanskrit can be an advantage.

Q: *Is the study group a subtle means of conversion to Hinduism?*

A: Not at all. Vedanta is not sectarian. As many study group members around the world have experienced, this study makes one a better individual irrespective of his faith and helps him understand more deeply the religion of his choice. Vedanta does not seek converts. It is a great catalyst for a deeper understanding of all the religions of the world. Its appeal is to the intellect and its application is universal. Hence it is used for personal growth and self-improvement and never for conversion.

Q: *Is chanting to be done in Sanskrit only?*

A: Since Vedanta was originally given out in the Sanskrit language, the chants also happen to be in Sanskrit. Hence they help us simulate the serene atmosphere of the early sages and masters. Although at first it may seem strange or difficult to chant in Sanskrit, hearing others chanting and enjoying the effect will ease the transition. If members who belong to different faiths wish to chant in their language, the group may decide to do so.

Q: *What if I don't like any of the other study group members?*

A: Likes and dislikes are inherent in human nature. Your study group will also have some people with whom you think you cannot get along. The message of Vedanta is far too precious for you to unnecessarily waste your own energy in petty likes and dislikes. An open mind and a little bit of tolerance will go a long way in helping you reap the full benefits of the study.

Q: *Does joining a study group require a fee?*

A: No, there is no fee for the study group. (If a study group forms around the study of the Chinmaya Lesson Course, the correspondence course does have a separate fee, paid by every subscriber to the course, whether he studies independently or in a group. The fee has nothing to do with the study group as such.)

Q: *Can I become a study group sevak in due course?*

A: Why not? If you have a good grasp of the subject matter, clear communication skills, unswerving enthusiasm, enough humility and sincerity to serve a cause, and, above all, perseverance, you have the right qualifications to be a sevak.

Q: *How can I join a study group in my area?*

A: Call (707) 247-3488 (or, using AT&T, 0-700-CHINMYA — 0-700-244-6692) for information about study groups in your area.

Q: *How can I subscribe to the Chinmaya Lesson Course?*

A: Call (707) 247-3488 (or, using AT&T, 0-700-CHINMYA — 0-700-244-6692) for information, or write directly to Chinmaya Lesson Course, CCMT, Sandeepany Sadhanalaya, Powai Park Drive, Bombay 400 072, India.

Appendix III
Scheme of Study

Book	First Reading	Number of times books are to be reviewed
Self-Unfoldment	10 pages	2
Bhaja Govindam	4 stanzas	2
Ātma Bodha	3 stanzas	3
Man-Making	12 pages	4
Meditation and Life	1 chapter	5
Nārada Bhakti Sutra	5 sutras	2
Gītā, Introduction	10 pages	3
We Must	10 pages	4
Kena Upaniṣad	2 mantras	3
Gītā, Chapters 1, 2, 3	3-5 stanzas	3
Kaṭha Upaniṣad	2 stanzas	3
Dakṣiṇāmūrti Stotram	2 mantras	3
Gītā, Chapters 4, 5, 6	3-5 stanzas	3
Īśāvāsyopaniṣad	3 mantras	3
Gītā, Chapters 7, 8, 9	3-5 stanzas	3

Book	**First Reading**	**Number of times books are to be reviewed**
Muṇḍaka Upaniṣad	2 mantras	3
Gītā, Chapters 10, 11	3-5 stanzas	3
Kaivalya Upaniṣad	2 mantras	3
Puruṣa Sūktam	2 stanzas	4
Gītā, Chapter 12	3-5 stanzas	3
Taittirīya Upaniṣad	2 mantras	3
Hymn to Badrinath	5 stanzas	3
Gītā, Chapters 13, 14, 15	3-5 stanzas	3
Aitareya Upaniṣad	3 mantras	3
Gītā, Chapters 16, 17	3-5 stanzas	3
Praśna Upaniṣad	2 mantras	4
Gītā, Chapter 18	3-5 stanzas	3
Ātma Bodha (repeat)	5 stanzas	3
Gītā, All Chapters (1-18)	5-10 stanzas	3
Aṣṭāvakra Gītā	3 verses	2
Māṇḍūkya Upaniṣad & Kārikā	2 mantras:	Read this book as many times as you can

Appendix IV

Guide to Sanskrit Transliteration and Pronunciation

Sanskrit is the language in which the teachings of Vedanta were first handed down orally, and later in written form. The language is thought to have originated from an early form of Aryan sometime around 2000 B.C. Later, in its perfected form, it became known as *Sanskrit*. The word Sanskrit is derived from the verb-root *kṛ* plus the prefix *sam*, meaning "to make perfect, to make complete."

The script used to write Sanskrit is Devanagari, which in the original means "divine city," being derived from two words, *deva*, "god, divine" and *nāgara*, "city."

The Sanskrit tradition is replete with spiritual literature from the earliest eras of Indian history. The Vedas, including the highly mystical literature of the Upanishads, all took form in the Sanskrit language. Even in current times, spiritual masters are known to write sacred literature in Sanskrit and at times even speak it. In *Self-Unfoldment*, as well as in many other books on the spiritual tradition of India, Sanskrit words are used abundantly, because in Sanskrit many terms were developed to describe spiritual concepts with utmost precision. Often, these Sanskrit terms have no precise equivalent in English, as, for instance, the words *māyā* (sometimes translated as "illusion") or *saṁsāra* (the endless cycle of births and deaths). Thus, in order to convey the most concise meaning possible, many teachers of Vedanta use the original Sanskrit terms in their teaching and writing, as Swami Chinmayananda has done in this book.

Sanskrit terms used in this book have been transliterated from the original Devanagari by using the international transliteration guidelines. These guidelines call for adding diacritical marks to English letters to guide the reader in correct pronunciation.

The following are the conventions used in *Self-Unfoldment.*

- Sanskrit words that appear within the text are printed in italic type, with diacritical marks.
- Commonly used Sanskrit words (such as *mantra* or *ashram*) have been incorporated into the English text and appear in roman type, without diacritical marks.
- Proper nouns derived from Sanskrit (such as *Vishnu* or *Upanishad*) have been incorporated into the English text in roman type, without diacritical marks. However, when those words appear as part of a Sanskrit phrase or title (such as *Taittirīya Upaniṣad*), the words appear in italic type, with diacritical marks.

The table on the following page provides an approximation of how Sanskrit letters are pronounced.

Pronunciation of Sanskrit Letters

a	but	k	skate	ḍ	no equivalent	m	much
ā	mom	kh	Kate	ḍh	no equivalent	y	young
i	it	g	gate	ṇ	no equivalent	r	drama
ī	beet	gh	gawk	t	tell	l	luck
u	put	ṅ	sing	th	time	v	wile/vile[1]
ū	pool	c	chunk	d	duck	ś	shove
ṛ	rrrrig	ch	match	dh	dumb	ṣ	bushel
e	play	j	John	n	numb	s	so
ai	high	jh	jam	p	spin	h	hum
o	toe	ñ	bunch	ph	pin		
au	cow	ṭ	no equivalent	b	bun		
		ṭh	no equivalent	bh	rub		

ṁ nasalization of preceding vowel

ḥ aspiration of preceding vowel

[1] The sound made by the Sanskrit letter *v* is a cross between the English *v* and *w*.

Glossary

Advaita	Nondualistic (monistic) Vedanta. Advaita Vedanta contends that the seeker and the Sought, the devotee and the Lord are one.
ahaṅkāra	Ego.
ahiṁsā	Noninjury at the mental level.
ānanda	Bliss. See also *sat-cit-ānanda*.
ānandamaya kośa	Bliss sheath, one of the five sheaths that encase the Self.
annamaya kośa	Food sheath, one of the five sheaths that encase the Self.
antaḥkaraṇa	Inner equipment; the mind-intellect.
apāna	In the vital-air sheath, the faculty of excretion, which controls the throwing out of excreta such as feces, urine, sperm, sputum, and perspiration.
āraṇyakas	Prescriptions for various methods of worship; one of the four main sections in each of the Vedas.

asatyam	Lack of truthfulness. See also *satyam*.
Atharva Veda	One of the four Vedas. See also *Vedas*.
Ātman	The Self, pure Consciousness, the immanent aspect of the supreme Reality. This same Consciousness, when regarded as transcendent, is called *Brahman*.
āvaraṇa	The veiling of Truth produced through the quality of *tamas*. See also *vikṣepa*.
avatāra (avatar)	Divine incarnation.
avidyā	Ignorance. Nonapprehension of the supreme Reality. Macrocosmic *avidyā* is called *māyā*.
Bhagavad Gītā	"Song of God." A major scriptural poem in eighteen chapters, contained in the *Mahābhārata*. It is a dialogue between Lord Krishna and Arjuna, his friend and disciple, on the battlefield of the dynastic war between the Pandavas and Kauravas.
bhakta	One who follows the path of devotion. See also *yoga*.
bhakti	Devotion. The path of devotion, one of the four main paths to liberation. See also *yoga*.
bhakti yoga	See *yoga*.
bhāvanā	An attitude or mood that one assumes toward the Divine.

Brahma — God in the aspect of Creator; one of the Hindu Trinity, the other two being Shiva and Vishnu.

brahmacārī — A seeker of the knowledge of *Brahman*; one who has taken the first monastic vows. The first of the four stages of life, the other being the life of the householder, the life of retirement, and renunciation. The feminine form of *brahmacārī* is *brahmacārini*.

brahmacarya — Continence in thought, word, and deed. Also the stage of the student, the first of the four stages into which an individual's life is divided. The status of a religious aspirant who has taken the first monastic vows.

Brahman — Pure Consciousness, the transcendent, all-pervading supreme Reality.

brāhmaṇas — Elaborate descriptions of rituals; one of the four main sections in each of the Vedas.

Brahma Sūtras — Vedantic aphorisms by Vyasa. Also known as *Vedānta Sūtras*.

brahmavidyā — Knowledge of *Brahman*; the science of infinite Reality.

brāhmin — Member of one of the four main castes, which includes priests, ministers, and subtle thinkers.

buddhi	The intellect; thoughts functioning as ideas, judgments, or decisions. See also *manas*.
cit	See *sat-cit-ānanda*.
citta	That aspect of the subtle body which makes our thoughts apparent to us.
dama	Self-control relative to the five sense organs.
deha vāsanās	The tendency to follow the urges of the body. See also *vāsanās*.
dharma	The inherent quality of anything, as the heat in fire and the sweetness in sugar. Righteousness; duty.
dhyāna	Meditation. See also *rāja yoga*.
duḥkha nivṛtti	Revulsion to sorrow, one of the two main motivators of human activity. See also *sukha prāpti*.
Dvaita	Dualism, propounded by Sri Madhvacharya, which contends that the devotee and the Lord are separate entities. See also *Advaita* and *Viśiṣṭādvaita*.
guṇa	Thought quality or texture. The three types of *guṇas* are: *sattva* (pure and serene), *rajas* (passionate and agitated), and *tamas* (dull and inactive).
	The preceptor-disciple or teacher-taught lineage.

guru-śiṣya-paramparā	The preceptor-disciple or teacher-taught lineage.
Hiraṇyagarbha	The supreme Reality manifesting as the Creator. Consciousness functioning through all minds and intellects.
indriyas	Sense organs. See also *jñāna indriyas* and *karma indriyas*.
Īśvara	The Lord, God. Consciousness functioning through *māyā*.
Īśvara darśana	"The vision of God." Recognition of the Self as one's true nature.
Itihāsas	"It so happened." Histories, including epics such as the *Mahābhārata* and the *Rāmāyaṇa*.
jagat	The universe.
japa, japa yoga	The training imparted to the mind by concentrating on a single line of thought to the exclusion of all other thoughts. It generally consists of repeating one of God's names, a mantra, with the help of a *mala*, a rosary.
jīva	The individual soul; the individuality or ego in a human being; *Ātman* identified with the body, mind, and senses.
jīvanmukta	One who has attained liberation while in the body.

jñāna	Divine Knowledge, wisdom. The path of knowledge, one of the four main paths to liberation. See also *yoga*.
jñāna indriyas	The five organs of perception: eyes, ears, nose, tongue, skin.
jñāna yoga	See *yoga*.
jñānī	One who follows the path of knowledge. Also, a liberated person, a knower of *Brahman*.
kāma	Desire.
karma	The sum of the effects of past actions; a sequence of cause and effect on the moral plane. Action, work.
karma indriyas	The five organs of action: hands, legs, organ of speech, genital organ, and organs of evacuation.
karma yoga	See *yoga*.
karma yogi	One who follows the path of action. See also *yoga*.
kośas	Sheaths, the external coatings of the Self: the food, vital-air, mental, intellectual, and bliss sheaths.
krodha	Anger.
kṣatriya	Member of one of the four main castes, which includes warriors, statesmen, and members of the ruling class.

Lakshmi	The Goddess of Wealth; the consort of Vishnu.
loka	World, field of experience, plane of existence.
loka vāsanās	The tendency that urges us to follow the patterns of the time. See also *vāsanās*.
Madhvacharya	A thirteenth-century exponent of Dualism (*Dvaita*). See also *Dvaita*.
Mahābhārata	A long epic poem, attributed to Vyasa, relating to the events of a dynastic war between the Pandavas and Kauravas. It illustrates the truths of the *Vedas* and includes the great philosophic poem, the *Bhagavad Gītā*.
mahatma	"Great Soul." A monk or highly advanced master.
mahāvākya	"Great statement." Aphoristic declarations of the supreme Truth; direct revelations of *Brahman*.
mala	Prayer beads used by the Hindus, generally consisting of 108 beads strung together on a single cord with a small space between the individual beads. One of the beads, called the *meru*, is left protruding.
manana	Reflection on and careful analysis of the knowledge gained from the teacher and the scriptures to render that knowledge free from doubt.

manas	Mind; thoughts in the form of emotions or in a state of restlessness. See also *buddhi*.
manomaya kośa	Mental sheath, one of the five sheaths that encase the Self.
mantra	A chosen name of God that a seeker repeats to himself to purify his mind.
mantras	Lyrical chants adoring the beauty of Nature, one of the four main sections in each of the Vedas.
māyā	Illusion; ignorance or nonapprehension of Reality. It is described as an inexplicable power inherent in the supreme Reality, as heat is inherent in fire.
meru	One of the 108 beads of the Hindu *mala*, which is left protruding to mark the end of one cycle of mantra-chanting. The *meru* is never crossed; when the *meru* is reached in the telling-of-the-beads, the *mala* is turned around and the rotation, along with the chanting, is resumed.
moha	Delusion.
mokṣa	Freedom from limitation (bondage); liberation from the cycle of birth and death.
mumukṣu	A seeker consumed by *mumukṣutva*, a burning desire for liberation.
mumukṣutva	An intense desire for liberation.

nāmarūpa	"Name and form." The apparent overlay of plurality over the nondual *Brahman*.
Narayana	A name of Vishnu.
neti neti	"Not this, not this." The approach of the discriminating mind toward the apparent reality of the phenomenal world; rejection of that reality as the not-Self.
nididyāsana	Meditation. The flow of like thoughts related to *Brahman*, to the exclusion of all other thoughts.
nirvikalpa samādhi	The transcendental state of consciousness in which the mind becomes totally absorbed in the supreme Reality, with all sense of individuality and duality lost. See also *savikalpa samādhi*.
niṣkāma karma	Desireless work without expectation of reward.
Om	Sometimes spelled *Aum*. Sacred syllable that represents the supreme Reality. Repetition of the syllable combined with meditation on its meaning is considered an effective spiritual practice.
pañca-kośa	The five sheaths that encase the Self: the food, vital-air, mental, intellectual, and bliss sheaths.
pañca-kośa viveka	"Discrimination of the five sheaths." The capacity to recognize the superimposed nature of the five sheaths and

	realize one's true nature as the Self. See also *pañca-kośas*.
pañca-prāṇas	The fivefold faculties of the vital-air sheath: perception (*prāṇa*), excretion (*apāna*), digestion (*samāna*), circulation (*vyāna*), and thinking (*udāna*).
pāpa	Sin; an action that causes us remorse and regret after we have acted with the wrong intention. See also *puṇya*.
Parvati	One of the forms of the Divine Mother; in other forms, also known as Uma and Shakti.
prakṛti	Matter, the material of the universe through which the Spirit (*Puruṣa*) manifests Itself. See also *Puruṣa*.
prāṇa	Primal energy from which mental and physical energies are evolved. In the vital-air sheath, the faculty of perception.
prāṇamaya kośa	Vital-air sheath, one of the five sheaths that encase the Self.
prārabdha	The principle of destiny. That portion of our past karmas which is being lived out in the present life.
prasthāna traya	Three texts describing the system of Vedanta, namely the Upanishads, the *Bhagavad Gītā*, and the *Brahma Sūtras*.
preyas	The path of the pleasant.

puṇya	Merit; meritorious action. An action that causes no regret but, instead, helps integrate our personality. See also *pāpa*.
Purāṇa	"Ancient." Any one of the 18 books of stories, attributed to Vyasa, in which Vedantic ideas are objectified and dramatized in the lives of saints, kings, devotees, and divine incarnations.
Puruṣa	Spirit, the pure Consciousness, which manifests Itself through *prakṛti*, matter. See also *prakṛti*.
puruṣārtha	Self-effort, a faculty unique to human beings, which helps them to choose their actions regardless of their inborn tendencies, the *vāsanās*.
rāga-dveṣa	Likes and dislikes.
rajas	One of the three thought textures (*guṇas*) that characterize the human personality. The *rājasic* quality is characterized by activity, passion, and agitation.
rāja yoga	A type of *yoga* expounded by Patanjali that focuses on concentration and meditation as a path. *Rāja yoga* has eight limbs: 1. *yama* (self-control) 2. *niyama* (observance of virtues) 3. *āsana* (postures) 4. *prāṇāyāma* (control of breath) 5. *pratyāhāra* (withdrawal of the mind) 6. *dhāraṇā* (concentration) 7. *dhyāna* (meditation) 8. *samādhi* (absorption)

Ramanuja	A twelfth-century philosopher-saint from South India, the founder of *Viśiṣṭādvaita*. See also *Viśiṣṭādvaita*.
Rāmāyaṇa	An ancient epic poem in Sanskrit written by the sage Valmiki, highlighting moral values through the life story of Sri Rama.
Ṛg Veda	One of the four Vedas. See also *Vedas*.
rishi	Sage, seer.
Ṣad Darśanas	The six schools of philosophy in India.
sādhanā	Any spiritual practice, such as reading the scriptures, meditating, distributing one's wealth to the needy, or withdrawing one's mind from worldly pursuits.
śama	Calmness of the mind; a condition experienced by the mind when it does not function in worldly activities.
samādhāna	Tranquillity of the mind; the poise the mind gains when it is trained to dwell continuously on a perfect ideal.
samādhi	"Tranquil mind." A state of absorption or thoughtlessness in which a person experiences his identity with the supreme Reality.
samāna	In the vital-air sheath, the faculty of digestion.
Sāma Veda	One of the four Vedas. See also *Vedas*.

saṁsāra	The endless cycle of births and deaths, of confusions and chaos, which human beings experience before they realize their identity with the supreme Reality.
Sanātana Dharma	"Eternal Way." The Hindu spiritual tradition. That truth which remains homogeneous and unchanging irrespective of time and place.
saṅga	Attachment.
sannyāsa	Renunciation; the monastic life. The last of the four stages of life, the other being student life (*brahmacarya*); married householder life (*gṛhastha*); and the life of retirement and contemplation (*vānaprastha*).
sannyāsī	A renunciate; one who has taken the vow of *sannyāsa*.
Sarasvati	Goddess of Knowledge; the consort of Brahma.
śāstra	Scriptures, including both those considered to be revealed by God (*Śruti*) and those written by sages (*Smṛti*).
śāstra vāsanās	The tendency to undertake mere scholarly study of various kinds of knowledge, either secular or religious. See also *vāsanās*.
sat	Existence. See also *sat-cit-ānanda*.
sat-cit-ānanda	Absolute existence-knowledge-bliss, an epithet for *Brahman*.

satsang (*satsaṇga*) — "Good company." Maintenance of contact with the higher values of life, either by association with noble persons or with inspiring writings and ideas.

sattva — One of the three thought textures (*guṇas*) that characterize the human personality. The *sāttvic* quality is characterized by purity and serenity.

satyam — Truthfulness; living in the spirit of our convictions.

savikalpa samādhi — The state of consciousness in which the mind experiences its essential divinity; at this stage, a trace of individuality still lingers to experience that divine vision. See also *nirvikalpa samādhi*.

Shakti — As a personification of primal energy, Shakti is the dynamic mother aspect of the supreme Reality. Also known in other forms, including Uma and Parvati.

Shankara — Also known as Shankaracharya and Adi Shankara. The greatest exponent of Advaita Vedanta (about the seventh century A.D.). He wrote extensive commentaries on the ten principal Upanishads, the *Brahma Sūtras*, and the *Bhagavad Gītā* and was the author of numerous texts on the fundamentals of Vedanta, including *Ātma Bodha*, *Bhaja Govindam*, and *Vivekacūḍāmaṇi*.

Shiva — God in the aspect of Destroyer; one of the Hindu Trinity, the other two being Vishnu and Brahma.

Smṛti	The body of traditional law, both religious and secular, that elaborates on the philosophic truths in the Upanishads.
śraddhā	Trust in the words of the teacher and the scriptures; faith in one's ideal.
śravaṇa	Listening to the teaching and engaging in the associated study of the scriptures in order to ascertain the reality of *Brahman*.
śreyas	The path of the good.
Śruti	"That which is heard." Scriptural teachings regarded as direct revelations from God to humanity; specifically, the Upanishads.
sthitaprajña	A person of steady wisdom, one established in the knowledge of the Self.
śudra	Member of the last of the four main castes, which includes laborers and servants.
sukha prāpti	Yearning for joy, one of the two main motivators of human activity. See also *duḥkha nivṛtti*.
tamas	One of the three thought textures (*guṇas*) that characterize the human personality. The *tāmasic* quality is characterized by dullness and inactivity.
titikṣa	Forbearance or silent endurance in the face of all obstacles.

Turīya	"The fourth." The fourth state of consciousness, which transcends the three ordinary states of consciousness—the waking, dreaming, and deep-sleep states.
udāna	In the vital-air sheath, the faculty of thinking. The capacity to entertain and absorb new thoughts.
Uma	Goddess of Matter; the consort of Shiva. Known in many forms, including Shakti and Parvati.
upādhi	Conditioning that is apparently imposed on *Ātman*, the pure Self, seemingly limiting it.
Upanishads *(Upaniṣads)*	The final, philosophic portion of each of the four Vedas; they constitute the quintessence of scriptural truths. In all, 108 Upanishads have been preserved.
uparati	Self-withdrawal, the quality of being unaffected by external disturbances.
upāsana	Worship.
vairāgya	Dispassion; indifference to worldly things.
vaiṣya	Member of one of the four main castes, which includes merchants and business people.
vāsanās	Inborn dispositions and motivating urges deep in the unconscious; the

	impressions formed in the personality when one acts in the world with egocentric desires.
Vedanta	"End of the Vedas." One of the six systems of Hindu philosophy, evolved from the Upanishads, the end portion of the Vedas. As the word *veda* means "knowledge," *Vedanta* can also denote "the end of knowledge" or "the most profound knowledge." Vedanta teaches that the purpose of our life is to realize the supreme Reality.
Vedas	Four ancient scriptural textbooks, compiled by the poet-sage Vyasa from prophetic declarations handed down from teacher to taught over many generations. The four books are the *Ṛg Veda*, the *Yajur Veda*, the *Sāma Veda*, and the *Atharva Veda*, each of which is divided into four sections: *mantras* (lyrical chants adoring the beauty of Nature); *brāhmaṇas* (elaborate descriptions of rituals); *āraṇyakas* (prescriptions for methods of subjective worship); *Upaniṣads* (philosophic declarations of the highest spiritual truths).
vidyā	Knowledge.
vijñānamaya kośa	Intellectual sheath, one of the five sheaths that encase the Self.
vikṣepa	Agitations in the mind (manifestations of *rajas*), resulting from the veiling (*āvaraṇa*) of the Truth. See also *āvaraṇa*.

Virāt	Consciousness functioning through the aggregate of all gross bodies.
Vishnu	God in the aspect of Preserver; one of the Hindu Trinity, the other two being Shiva and Brahma.
Viśiṣṭādvaita	Qualified Monism, expounded by Sri Ramanuja, which contends that the devotee is part of the whole, the Lord.
viveka	Discrimination between the ephemeral objects of the world and the eternal Principle of life.
vyāna	In the vital-air sheath, the faculty of circulation.
Vyasa	Also known as Veda Vyasa. The poet-seer who compiled the Vedas and the *Brahma Sūtras*. The epic *Mahābhārata* (which contains the *Bhagavad Gītā*) and the *Purāṇas* are also attributed to him.
Yajur Veda	One of the four Vedas. See also *Vedas*.
yoga	The word *yoga* comes from the root *yuj*, "to join, to yoke." The joining of the self to the supreme Self. Also the techniques that promote one's progress toward the realization of the Supreme. Four of the major yogas (techniques, paths) are: 1. *Bhakti yoga*, the path of devotion, is the most fitting path for those whose heart is relatively more developed than the head. A *bhakta* is one who follows the path of devotion.

2. *Hatha yoga* deals primarily with the control of breath and the culture of the body through a system of physical exercises and postures.

3. *Jñāna yoga*, the path of knowledge, is the most fitting path for those whose head is more developed than the heart. Through discrimination, the seeker differentiates between the Real and the unreal and finally comes to realize his identity with the supreme Reality. A *jñānī* is a follower of the path of knowledge.

4. *Karma yoga*, the path of action, is most fitting for those of mixed temperament—whose head and heart are equally developed. The seeker performs selfless activity, dedicating all his actions to a higher ideal and giving up all sense of agency. A *karma yogi* is a selfless worker who follows the path of action.

yogi — One who practices yoga. The feminine form of *yogi* is *yogini*.

Bibliography

Aitareya Upanishad (*Aitareya Upaniṣad*). Commentary by Swami Chinmayananda. Bombay, India: Central Chinmaya Mission Trust, 1982.

Chinmayananda, Swami. *Meditation and Life*. Piercy, California: Chinmaya Publications West, 1992.

Chinmayananda, Swami. *We Must*. Napa, California: Chinmaya Publications West, 1976.

Holy Geeta, The (*Bhagavad Gītā*). Commentary by Swami Chinmayananda. Bombay, India: Central Chinmaya Mission Trust, 1980.

Isavasya Upanishad (*Īśāvāsya Upaniṣad*). Commentary by Swami Chinmayananda. Bombay, India: Central Chinmaya Mission Trust, 1980.

Katha Upanishad (*Kaṭha Upaniṣad*). Commentary by Swami Chinmayananda. Bombay, India: Central Chinmaya Mission Trust, 1989.

Mundaka Upanishad (*Muṇḍaka Upaniṣad*). Commentary by Swami Chinmayananda. Bombay, India: Central Chinmaya Mission Trust, 1973.

Nārada Bhakti Sūtra. Commentary by Swami Chinmayananda. Bombay, India: Central Chinmaya Mission Trust, 1990.

Question of Freedom, The. Mananam Publication Series, Volume X: Number 2. Piercy, California: Chinmya Mission West, 1987.

Shankaracharya. *Ātma Bodha*. Commentary by Swami Chinmayananda. Bombay, India: Central Chinmaya Mission Trust, 1987.

Shankaracharya. *Bhaja Govindam*. Commentary by Swami Chinmayananda. Bombay, India: Central Chinmaya Mission Trust, 1990.

Shankaracharya. *Vivekachoodamani* (*Vivekacūḍāmaṇi*). Commentary by Swami Chinmayananda. Bombay, India: Central Chinmaya Mission Trust, 1987.

Tapovanam, Swami. *Guidance from the Guru*. Bombay, India: Central Chinmaya Mission Trust, 1976.

Tapovanam, Swami. *Wanderings in the Himalayas*. Bombay, India: Central Chinmaya Mission Trust, 1981.

About the Author

Swami Chinmayananda (1916-1993) dedicated his life to creating a renaissance of spiritual and cultural values in the country of his birth, India. He is often compared to Adi Shankaracharya, the greatest exponent of Vedanta, who thirteen centuries ago brought about a spiritual revival in India.

Born in 1916 in Kerala, India, Swami Chinmayananda was a world-renowned authority on the scriptures of India, especially the *Bhagavad Gītā* and the Upanishads. The year 1993, when he attained *Mahasamādhi* and passed from the physical plane of existence, marked forty-one years of his work as a teacher of Vedanta, a tradition of teaching that unfolds the underlying philosophic principles behind all the major religions of the world. Since the mid-sixties, his talk series, called *yajñas*, had been enjoyed worldwide, as he lectured throughout the United States, Canada, Europe, the Middle East, the Far East, Australia, and Africa.

Swami Chinmayananda began his study of Vedanta as a skeptical journalist under the tutelage of Swami Sivananda and Swami Tapovanam. His studies finished, he returned to the teeming cities of India to expound the ancient scriptural texts in English to college students, business people, and the public at large. He was the head of a worldwide organization called Chinmaya Mission, which was his vehicle for not only spreading the message of Vedanta but also for overseeing numerous cultural, educational, and social-service activities such as: the publication of books and audio and video tapes; institutes of Vedantic study; ashrams; the sponsoring of seminars, lecture series, and spiritual retreats across the globe; and the administration of schools, hospitals, orphanages, homes for the elderly, forest sanctuaries, and village improvement projects. Swami Tejomayananda, one of Swami Chinmayananda's senior disciples, is now continuing his guru's work as head of Chinmaya Mission worldwide.

Swami Chinmayananda started out his life as Balakrishna Menon in South India, in the state of Kerala, as the eldest son of a prominent judge. After finishing his intermediate studies in science at Maharaja College in Ernakulam, he went to Trichur to study arts at St. Thomas College. Thereafter, he attended Madras University and was graduated in 1939 with degrees in science and political science. He then went to Lucknow in North India to take postgraduate degrees in literature and law. After graduation, Balakrishna Menon chose journalism rather than law as his career. He joined Nehru's newspaper, the *National Herald*, becoming a regular feature writer. While working at the *National Herald*, he actively joined India's independence movement and was imprisoned. In prison, he became seriously ill and was transferred to a hospital, where he chanced upon some articles by Swami Sivananda, which aroused both his interest and his skepticism.

After his release from prison, Balakrishna Menon went to the Himalayas to seek out Swami Sivananda, though he later said, "I went not to gain knowledge but to find out how the swamis were keeping up the bluff among the masses." In the Himalayas, the young skeptic turned enthusiast and finally renunciate monk, assuming the monastic name of Swami Chinmayananda. Soon thereafter, he sought out one of the greatest Vedantic masters of his time, Swami Tapovanam of Uttarkashi, and devoted the next several years of his life to an intensive study of the scriptures.

Swami Chinmayananda is the author of more than thirty books on Vedanta, most of them published in India. In the summer of 1991 he completed a video-taped commentary on the complete *Bhagavad Gītā*, which spans more than one hundred hours of lectures held at a Chinmaya Mission center of study and work called Krishnalaya, in Piercy, California.

Other Books by Swami Chinmayananda

Introductory Books

Art of Living
Art of Man-Making
I Love You
Kindle Life
Meditation and Life
Satsang with Swami Chinmayananda
Vedanta through Letters
We Must

Commentaries on Texts by Shankara

Atma Bodha
Bhaja Govindam
Forgive Me (Sivaparadhaksamapanastotram)
Hymn to Dakshinamoorthy
Sadhana Panchakam
Vakya Vritti
Vivekachoodamani

Commentaries on the Major Upanishads

Aitareya Upanishad
Isavasya Upanishad
Kaivalya Upanishad
Katha Upanishad
Kena Upanishad
Mandukya Upanishad (and Karika)
Mundaka Upanishad
Prasna Upanishad
Taittiriya Upanishad

Miscellaneous Texts

Art of Meditation
Ashtavakra Geeta
Geeta for Children
Holy Geeta, The
Maya and Maneesha Panchakam
Meditation, Gateway to Freedom
My Trek through Uttarkhand
Narada Bhakti Sutra
Purusha Sooktam
Vishnu Sahasranama (with commentary)

Books Translated into Other Languages

Hindi

Atma Vikaski Nirdeshak
Atma Bodha
Holy Geeta, The
Manav Nirmana Kala

Telegu

Atma Bodha
Bhaja Govindam
Dhyanamu-Jeevitamu
Holy Geeta, The
Katha Upanishad
Mandukya Upanishad (and Karika)
Mundaka Upanishad

Gujarati

Atma Bodha
Bhaja Govindam
Geeta, Vol. I
Geeta, Vol. II
Geeta, Vol. III
Geeta, Vol. IV
Jeevan Jyoti Jalao (Kindle Life)
Jeevan Vikas Marg Darsan (Self-Unfoldment)
Kshama Karo

Index

A

H

I

J

K

L

M

U

V